When Hitler Stole Pink Rabbit

Suppose your country began to change. Suppose that without your noticing, it became dangerous for some people to live in any longer. Suppose you found, to your complete surprise, that your own father was one of those people.

That is what happened to Anna, in Germany in 1933.

She was nine years old when it began, too busy with her schoolwork and tobogganing to take much notice of political posters, but out of them glared the face of Adolf Hitler, the man who would soon change the whole of Europe—starting with her own small life.

Anna suddenly found things moving too fast for her to understand. One day her father was unaccountably, frighteningly, missing. Then she herself and her brother Max were being rushed by their mother in alarming secrecy away from everything they knew—home and schoolmates and well-loved toys—right out of Germany.

In a foreign land the family was reunited, moving into a huge adventure that was to go on for years through country after country. For Anna and Max it meant learning all the way—new languages and peoples, how to pick their way through the wildest confusions and how to be poor. There were special skills to being a refugee, Anna discovered, and against all expectations she could actually enjoy them. So long as the family stayed together, that was all that mattered. Tight together, nothing mattered. But if anything should crack them apart . . .

Judith Kerr is already well known for her children's picture books. With this delightful and moving novel for older readers, she breaks new ground. Perhaps not quite a novel. Most of it is true.

When Hitler Stole Pink Rabbit

JUDITH KERR

Illustrated by the author

COLLINS

St James's Place, London

ISBN 0 00 184913 1

© *Judith Kerr 1971*
First published 1971
Reprinted 1974
Printed in Great Britain
Collins Clear-Type Press
London and Glasgow

For my parents
Julia and Alfred Kerr

Chapter One

Anna was walking home from school with Elsbeth, a girl in
her class. A lot of snow had fallen in Berlin that winter. It
did not melt, so the street cleaners had swept it to the edge of
the pavement, and there it had lain for weeks in sad, greying
heaps. Now, in February, the snow had turned into slush and
there were puddles everywhere. Anna and Elsbeth skipped
over them in their lace-up boots.

They both wore thick coats and woollen caps which kept
their ears warm, and Anna had a muffler as well. She was nine
but small for her age and the ends of the muffler hung down
almost to her knees. It also covered up her mouth and nose,
so the only parts of her that showed were her green eyes and a
tuft of dark hair. She had been hurrying because she wanted
to buy some crayons at the paper shop and it was nearly time

for lunch. But now she was so out of breath that she was glad when Elsbeth stopped to look at a large red poster.

"It's another picture of that man," said Elsbeth. "My little sister saw one yesterday and thought it was Charlie Chaplin."

Anna looked at the staring eyes, the grim expression. She said, "It's not a bit like Charlie Chaplin except for the moustache."

They spelled out the name under the photograph.

Adolf Hitler.

"He wants everybody to vote for him in the elections and then he's going to stop the Jews," said Elsbeth. "Do you think he's going to stop Rachel Lowenstein?"

"Nobody can stop Rachel Lowenstein," said Anna. "She's form captain. Perhaps he'll stop me. I'm Jewish too."

"You're not!"

"I am! My father was talking to us about it only last week. He said we were Jews and no matter what happened my brother and I must never forget it."

"But you don't go to a special church on Saturdays like Rachel Lowenstein."

"That's because we're not religious. We don't go to church at all."

"I wish my father wasn't religious," said Elsbeth. "We have to go every Sunday and I get cramp in my seat." She looked at Anna curiously. "I thought Jews were supposed to have bent noses, but your nose is quite ordinary. Has your brother got a bent nose?"

"No," said Anna. "The only person in our house with a bent nose is Bertha the maid, and hers only got like that because she broke it falling off a tram."

Elsbeth was getting annoyed. "Well then," she said, "if you look the same as everyone else and you don't go to a special church, how do you know you *are* Jewish? How can you be sure?"

There was a pause.

"I suppose . . ." said Anna, "I suppose it's because my

8

mother and father are Jews, and I suppose their mothers and fathers were too. I never thought about it much until Papa started talking about it last week."

"Well, I think it's silly!" said Elsbeth. "It's silly about Adolf Hitler and people being Jews and everything!" She started to run and Anna followed her.

They did not stop until they reached the paper shop. There was someone talking to the man at the counter and Anna's heart sank as she recognised Fraulein Lambeck who lived nearby. Fraulein Lambeck was making a face like a sheep and saying, "Terrible times! Terrible times!" Each time she said "terrible times" she shook her head and her ear-rings wobbled.

The paper shop man said, "1931 was bad enough, 1932 was worse, but mark my words, 1933 will be worst of all." Then he saw Anna and Elsbeth and said, "What can I do for you, my dears?"

Anna was just going to tell him that she wanted to buy some crayons when Fraulein Lambeck spied her.

"It's little Anna!" cried Fraulein Lambeck. "How are you, little Anna? And how is your dear father? Such a wonderful man! I read every word he writes. I've got all his books and I always listen to him on the radio. But he hasn't written anything in the paper this week—I do hope he's quite well. Perhaps he's lecturing somewhere. Oh, we do need him in these terrible, terrible times!"

Anna waited until Fraulein Lambeck had finished. Then she said, "He's got 'flu."

This provoked another outburst. You would have thought that Fraulein Lambeck's nearest and dearest were lying at death's door. She shook her head until the ear-rings rattled. She suggested remedies. She recommended doctors. She would not stop talking until Anna had promised to give her father Fraulein Lambeck's best wishes for a speedy recovery. And then she turned back in the doorway and said, "Don't say best wishes from Fraulein Lambeck, little Anna—just say from an admirer!"—before she finally swept out.

Anna bought her crayons quickly. Then she and Elsbeth stood together in the cold wind outside the paper shop. This was where their ways normally parted, but Elsbeth lingered. There was something she had wanted to ask Anna for a long time and it seemed a good moment.

"Anna," said Elsbeth, "is it nice having a famous father?"

"Not when you meet someone like Fraulein Lambeck," said Anna, absent-mindedly setting off for home while Elsbeth equally absent-mindedly followed her.

"No, but apart from Fraulein Lambeck?"

"I think it's quite nice. For one thing Papa works at home, so we see quite a lot of him. And sometimes we get free theatre tickets. And once we were interviewed by a newspaper, and they asked us what books we liked, and my brother said Zane Grey and the next day someone sent him a whole set as a present!"

"I wish my father was famous," said Elsbeth. "But I don't think he ever will be because he works in the Post Office, and that's not the sort of thing people get famous for."

"If your father doesn't become famous perhaps you will. One snag about having a famous father is that you almost never become famous yourself."

"Why not?"

"I don't know. But you hardly ever hear of two famous people in the same family. It makes me rather sad sometimes." Anna sighed.

By this time they were standing outside Anna's white-painted gate. Elsbeth was feverishly trying to think of something she might become famous for when Heimpi who had seen them from the window opened the front door.

"Goodness!" cried Elsbeth, "I'll be late for lunch!"—and she rushed off up the street.

"You and that Elsbeth," grumbled Heimpi as Anna went inside. "You'd talk the monkeys off the trees!"

Heimpi's real name was Fraulein Heimpel and she had looked after Anna and her brother Max since they were babies.

Now that they were older she did the housekeeping while they were at school, but she liked to fuss over them when they came back. "Let's have all this off you," she said, unwinding the muffler. "You look like a parcel with the string undone." As Heimpi peeled the clothes off her Anna could hear the piano being played in the drawing room. So Mama was home.

"Are you sure your feet aren't wet?" said Heimpi. "Then go quickly and wash your hands. Lunch is nearly ready."

Anna climbed up the thickly carpeted stairs. The sun was shining through the window and outside in the garden she could see a few last patches of snow. The smell of chicken drifted up from the kitchen. It was nice coming home from school.

As she opened the bathroom door there was a scuffle inside and she found herself staring straight at her brother Max, his face scarlet under his fair hair, his hands hiding something behind his back.

"What's the matter?" she asked, even before she caught sight of his friend Gunther who seemed equally embarrassed.

"Oh, it's you!" said Max, and Gunther laughed, "We thought it was a grown-up!"

"What have you got?" asked Anna.

"It's a badge. There was a big fight at school today—Nazis against Sozis."

"What are Nazis and Sozis?"

"I'd have thought even you would know that at your age," said Max who was just twelve. "The Nazis are the people who are going to vote for Hitler in the elections. We Sozis are the people who are going to vote against."

"But you're none of you allowed to vote," said Anna. "You're too young!"

"Our fathers, then," said Max crossly. "It's the same thing."

"Anyway, we beat them," said Gunther. "You should have seen those Nazis run! Max and I caught one of them and got his badge off him. But I don't know what my Mum is going to say about my trousers." He looked dolefully down at a large tear in the worn cloth. Gunther's father was out of work and there was no money at home for new clothes.

11

"Don't worry, Heimpi will fix it," said Anna. "Can I see the badge?"

It was a small piece of red enamel with a black hooked cross on it.

"It's called a swastika," said Gunther. "All the Nazis have them."

"What are you going to do with it?"

Max and Gunther looked at each other.

"D'you want it?" asked Max.

Gunther shook his head. "I'm not supposed to have anything to do with the Nazis. My Mum's afraid I might get my head cut open."

"They don't fight fair," agreed Max. "They use sticks and stones and everything." He turned the badge over with increasing dislike. "Well, I certainly don't want it."

"Put it down the what-not!" said Gunther. So they did. The first time they pulled the chain it would not flush away, but the second time, just as the gong went for lunch, it disappeared very satisfactorily.

They could still hear the piano as they went downstairs but it stopped while Heimpi was filling their plates and a moment later the door burst open and Mama came in.

"Hullo children, hullo Gunther," she cried, "how was school?"

Everybody immediately began to tell her and the room was suddenly filled with noise and laughter. She knew the names of all their teachers and always remembered what they had told her. So when Max and Gunther talked about how the Geography master had flown into a rage she said, "No wonder, after the way you all played him up last week!" And when Anna told her that her essay had been read out in class she said, "That's marvellous—because Fraulein Schmidt hardly ever reads anything out, does she?"

When she listened she looked at whoever was talking with the utmost concentration. When she talked all her energy went into it. She seemed to do everything twice as hard as other people—even her eyes were a brighter blue than any Anna had ever seen.

They were just starting on the pudding which was apple strudel when Bertha the maid came in to tell Mama that there was someone on the telephone, and should she disturb Papa?

"What a time to ring up!" cried Mama and pushed her chair back so hard that Heimpi had to put out her hand to stop it falling over. "Don't any of you dare eat my apple strudel!" And she rushed out.

It seemed very quiet after she had gone though Anna could hear her footsteps hurrying to the telephone and, a little later, hurrying even faster up the stairs to Papa's room. In the silence she asked, "How is Papa?"

"Feeling better," said Heimpi. "His temperature is down a bit."

Anna ate her pudding contentedly. Max and Gunther got through three helpings but still Mama had not come back. It was odd because she was particularly fond of apple strudel.

Bertha came to clear away and Heimpi took the boys off to see to Gunther's trousers. "No use mending these," she said, "they'd split again as soon as you breathed. But I've got an outgrown pair of Max's that will just do you nicely."

Anna was left in the dining-room wondering what to do. For a while she helped Bertha. They put the used plates through the hatch into the pantry. Then they brushed the crumbs off the table with a little brush and pan. Then, while they were folding up the table cloth, she remembered Fraulein Lambeck and her message. She waited until Bertha had the table cloth safely in her hands and ran up to Papa's room. She could hear Papa and Mama talking inside.

"Papa," said Anna as she opened the door, "I met Fraulein Lambeck . . ."

"Not now! Not now!" cried Mama. "We're talking!" She was sitting on the edge of Papa's bed. Papa was propped up against the pillows looking rather pale. They were both frowning.

"But Papa, she asked me to tell you . . ."

13

Mama got quite angry.

"For goodness sake, Anna," she shouted, "we don't want to hear about it now! Go away!"

"Come back a little later," said Papa more gently. Anna shut the door. So much for that! It wasn't as though she'd ever wanted to deliver Fraulein Lambeck's silly message in the first place. But she felt put out.

There was no one in the nursery. She could hear shouts outside, so Max and Gunther were probably playing in the garden, but she did not feel like joining them. Her satchel was hanging on the back of a chair. She unpacked her new crayons and took them all out of their box. There was a good pink and quite a good orange, but the blues were best. There were three different shades, all beautifully bright, and a purple as well. Suddenly Anna had an idea.

Lately she had been producing a number of illustrated poems which had been much admired both at home and at school. There had been one about a fire, one about an earthquake and one about a man who died in dreadful agonies after being cursed by a tramp. Why not try her hand at a shipwreck? All sorts of words rhymed with sea and there was "save" to rhyme with "wave", and she could use the three new blue crayons for the illustration. She found some paper and began.

Soon she was so absorbed that she did not notice the early winter dusk creeping into the room, and she was startled when Heimpi came in and switched on the light.

"I've made some cakes," said Heimpi. "Do you want to help with the icing?"

"Can I just quickly show this to Papa?" asked Anna as she filled in the last bit of blue sea. Heimpi nodded.

This time Anna knocked and waited until Papa called "Come in". His room looked strange because only the bedside lamp was lit and Papa and his bed made an island of light among the shadows. She could dimly see his desk with the typewriter and the mass of papers which had, as usual, overflowed from the desk on to the floor. Because Papa often wrote late at night and did not want to disturb Mama his bed was in his workroom.

Papa himself did not look like someone who was feeling better. He was sitting up doing nothing at all, just staring in front of him with a kind of tight look on his thin face, but when he saw Anna he smiled. She showed him the poem and he read it through twice and said it was very good, and he also admired the illustration. Then Anna told him about Fraulein Lambeck and they both laughed. He was looking more like himself, so Anna said, "Papa, do you really like the poem?"

Papa said he did.

"You don't think it should be more cheerful?"

"Well," said Papa, "a shipwreck is not really a thing you can be very cheerful about."

"My teacher Fraulein Schmidt thinks I should write about more cheerful subjects like the spring and the flowers."

"And do you want to write about the spring and the flowers?"

"No," said Anna sadly. "Right now all I seem to be able to do is disasters."

Papa gave a little sideways smile and said perhaps she was in tune with the times.

"Do you think then," asked Anna anxiously, "that disasters are all right to write about?" Papa became serious at once.

"Of course!" he said. "If you want to write about disasters, that's what you must do. It's no use trying to write what other people want. The only way to write anything good is to try to please yourself."

Anna was so encouraged to hear this that she was just going to ask Papa whether by any chance Papa thought she might become famous one day, but the telephone by Papa's bed rang loudly and surprised them both.

The tight look was back on Papa's face as he lifted the receiver and it was odd, thought Anna, how even his voice sounded different. She listened to him saying, "Yes . . . yes . . ." and something about Prague before she lost interest. But the conversation was soon over.

"You'd better run along now," said Papa. He lifted his

15

arms as though to give her a big hug. Then he put them down again. "I'd better not give you my 'flu," he said.

Anna helped Heimpi ice the cakes and then she and Max and Gunther ate them—all except three which Heimpi put in a paper bag for Gunther to take home to his Mum. She had also found some more of Max's outgrown clothes to fit him, so he had quite a nice parcel to take with him when he left.

They spent the rest of the evening playing games. Max and Anna had been given a games compendium for Christmas and had not yet got over the wonder of it. It contained draughts, chess, Ludo, Snakes and Ladders, dominoes and six different card games, all in one beautifully made box. If you got tired of one game you could always play another. Heimpi sat with them in the nursery mending socks and even joined them for a game of Ludo. Bed-time came far too soon.

Next morning before school Anna ran into Papa's room to see him. The desk was tidy. The bed was neatly made.

Papa had gone.

Chapter Two

Anna's first thought was so terrible that she could not breathe. Papa had got worse in the night. He had been taken to hospital. Perhaps he . . . She ran blindly out of the room and found herself caught by Heimpi.

"It's all right!" said Heimpi. "It's all right! Your father has gone on a journey."

"A journey?" Anna could not believe it. "But he's ill—he had a temperature . . ."

"He decided to go just the same," said Heimpi firmly. "Your mother was going to explain it all to you when you came home from school. Now I suppose you'll have to hear straight away and Fraulein Schmidt will be kept twiddling her thumbs for you."

"What is it? Are we going to miss school?" Max appeared hopefully on the landing.

Then Mama came out of her room. She was still in her dressing-gown and looked tired.

"There's no need to get terribly excited," she said. "But there are some things I must tell you. Heimpi, shall we have some coffee? And I expect the children could eat some more breakfast."

Once they were all settled in Heimpi's pantry with coffee and rolls Anna felt much better and was even able to calculate that she would miss the geography lesson at school which she particularly disliked.

"It's quite simple," said Mama. "Papa thinks Hitler and the Nazis might win the elections. If that happened he would not want to live in Germany while they were in power, and nor would any of us."

"Because we're Jews?" asked Anna.

"Not only because we're Jews. Papa thinks no one would be allowed to say what they thought any more, and he wouldn't be able to write. The Nazis don't like people to disagree with them." Mama drank some of her coffee and looked more cheerful. "Of course it may never happen and if it did it probably wouldn't last for long—maybe six months or so. But at the moment we just don't know."

"But why did Papa leave so suddenly?" asked Max.

"Because yesterday someone rang him up and warned him that they might be going to take away his passport. So I packed him a small suitcase and he caught the night train to Prague—that's the quickest way out of Germany."

"Who could take away his passport?"

"The Police. There are quite a few Nazis in the Police."

"And who rang him up to warn him?"

Mama smiled for the first time.

"Another policeman. One Papa had never met—but who had read his books and liked them."

It took Anna and Max some time to digest all this.

Then Max asked, "But what's going to happen now?"

"Well," said Mama, "it's only about ten days until the elections. Either the Nazis lose, in which case Papa comes back —or they win, in which case we join him."

"In Prague?" asked Max.

"No, probably in Switzerland. They speak German there— Papa would be able to write. We'd probably rent a little house and stay there until all this has blown over."

"Heimpi too?" asked Anna.

"Heimpi too."

It sounded quite exciting. Anna was beginning to imagine it—a house in the mountains . . . goats . . . or was it cows? . . . when Mama said, "There is one thing more." Her voice was very serious.

"This is the most important thing of all," said Mama, "and we need you to help us with it. Papa does not want anyone to know that he has left Germany. So you must not tell anyone. If anyone asks you about him you must say that he's still in bed with 'flu."

"Can't I even tell Gunther?" asked Max.

"No. Not Gunther, not Elsbeth, not anyone."

"All right," said Max. "But it won't be easy. People are always asking after him."

"Why can't we tell anyone?" asked Anna. "Why doesn't Papa want anyone to know?"

"Look," said Mama. "I've explained it all to you as well as I can. But you're both still children—you can't understand everything. Papa thinks the Nazis might . . . cause us some bother if they knew that he'd gone. So he does not want you to talk about it. Now are you going to do what he asks or not?"

Anna said, yes, of course she would.

Then Heimpi bundled them both off to school. Anna was worried about what to say if anyone asked her why she was late, but Max said, "Just tell them Mama overslept—she did, anyway!"

In fact no one was very interested. They did high-jump in Gym and Anna jumped higher than anyone else in her class.

She was so pleased about this that for the rest of the morning she almost forgot about Papa being in Prague.

When it was time to go home it all came back to her and she hoped Elsbeth would not ask her any awkward questions—but Elsbeth's mind was on more important matters. Her aunt was coming to take her out that afternoon to buy her a yo-yo. What kind did Anna think she should choose? And what colour? The wooden ones worked best on the whole, but Elsbeth had seen a bright orange one which, though made of tin, had so impressed her with its beauty that she was tempted. Anna only had to say Yes and No, and by the time she got home for lunch the day felt more ordinary than she would ever have thought possible that morning.

Neither Anna nor Max had any homework and it was too cold to go out, so in the afternoon they sat on the radiator in the nursery and looked out of the window. The wind was rattling the shutters and blowing great lumps of cloud across the sky.

"We might get more snow," said Max.

"Max," said Anna, "do you hope that we will go to Switzerland?"

"I don't know," said Max. There were so many things he would miss. Gunther . . . his gang with whom he played football . . . school . . . He said, "I suppose we'd go to a school in Switzerland."

"Oh yes," said Anna. "I think it would be quite fun." She was almost ashamed to admit it, but the more she thought about it the more she wanted to go. To be in a strange country where everything would be different—to live in a different house, go to a different school with different children—a huge urge to experience it all overcame her and though she knew it was heartless a smile appeared on her face.

"It would only be for six months," she said apologetically, "and we'd all be together."

The next few days passed fairly normally. Mama got a letter from Papa. He was comfortably installed in a hotel in Prague and was feeling much better. This cheered everyone up.

A few people enquired after him but were quite satisfied when the children said he had 'flu. There was so much of it about that it was not surprising. The weather continued very cold and the puddles caused by the thaw all froze hard again—but still there was no snow.

At last on the afternoon of the Sunday before the elections the sky turned very dark and then suddenly opened up to release a mass of floating, drifting, whirling white. Anna and Max were playing with the Kentner children who lived across the road. They stopped to watch the snow come down.

"If only it had started a bit earlier," said Max. "By the time it's thick enough for tobogganing, it will be too dark."

At five o'clock when Anna and Max were going home it had only just stopped. Peter and Marianne Kentner saw them to the door. The snow lay thick and dry and crunchy all over the road and the moon was shining down on it.

"Why don't we go tobogganing in the moonlight?" said Peter.

"Do you think they'd let us?"

"We've done it before," said Peter who was fourteen. "Go and ask your mother."

Mama said they could go provided they all stayed together and got home by seven. They put on their warmest clothes and set off.

It was only a quarter of an hour's walk to the Grunewald, where a wooded slope made an ideal run down to a frozen lake. They had tobogganed there many times before, but it had always been daylight and the air had been loud with the shouts of other children. Now all they could hear was the soughing of the wind in the trees, the crunching of the new snow under their feet, and the gentle whir of the sledges as they slid along behind them. Above their heads the sky was dark but the ground shone blue in the moonlight and the shadows of the trees broke like black bands across it.

At the top of the slope they stopped and looked down. Nobody had been on it before them. The shimmering path of

21

snow stretched ahead, perfect and unmarked, right down to the edge of the lake.

"Who's going down first?" asked Max.

Anna did not mean to, but she found herself hopping up and down and saying, "Oh please—please . . .!"

Peter said, "All right—youngest first."

That meant her because Marianne was ten.

She sat on her sledge, held on to the steering rope, took a deep breath and pushed off. The sledge began to move, rather gently, down the hill.

"Go on!" shouted the boys behind her. "Give it another push!"

But she didn't. She kept her feet on the runners and let the sledge gather speed slowly. The powdery snow sprayed up all round her as the sledge struck it. The trees moved past, slowly at first, then faster and faster. The moonlight leapt all round her. At last she seemed to be flying through a mass of silver. Then the sledge hit the hump at the bottom of the slope, shot across it, and landed in a dapple of moonlight on the frozen lake. It was beautiful.

The others came down after her, squealing and shouting.

They went down the slope head first on their stomachs so that the snow sprayed straight into their faces. They went down feet first on their backs with the black tops of the fir trees rushing past above them. They all squeezed on to one sledge together and came down so fast that they shot on almost to the middle of the lake. After each ride they struggled back up the slope, panting and pulling the sledges behind them. In spite of the cold they were steaming inside their woollies.

Then it began to snow again. At first they hardly noticed it, but then the wind got up and blew the snow in their faces. All at once Max stopped in the middle of dragging his sledge up the slope and said, "What time is it? Oughtn't we to be getting back?"

Nobody had a watch and they suddenly realised that they had no idea how long they had been there. Perhaps it was quite late and their parents had been waiting for them at home.

"Come on," said Peter. "We'd better go quickly." He took off his gloves and knocked them together to shake the caked snow off them. His hands were red with cold. So were Anna's, and she noticed for the first time that her feet were frozen.

It was chilly going back. The wind blew through their damp clothes and with the moon hidden behind the clouds the path was black in front of them. Anna was glad when they were out of the trees and in a road. Soon there were street lamps, houses with lighted windows, shops. They were nearly home.

An illuminated clockface showed them the time. After all it was not yet quite seven. They heaved sighs of relief and walked more slowly. Max and Peter began to talk about football. Marianne tied two sledges together and scampered wildly ahead on the empty road, leaving a network of overlapping tracks in the snow. Anna lagged behind because her cold feet hurt.

She could see the boys stop outside her house, still talking and waiting for her, and was just going to catch them up, when she heard the creak of a gate. Something moved in the path beside her and suddenly a shapeless figure loomed up. For a moment she was very frightened—but then she saw that it was only Fraulein Lambeck in some sort of a furry cloak and with a letter in her hand.

"Little Anna!" cried Fraulein Lambeck. "Fancy meeting you in the dark of the night! I was just going to the post box but did not think to find a kindred spirit. And how is your dear Papa?"

"He's got 'flu," said Anna automatically.

Fraulein Lambeck stopped in her tracks.

"Still got 'flu, little Anna? You told me he had 'flu a week ago."

"Yes," said Anna.

"And he's still in bed? Still got a temperature?"

"Yes," said Anna.

"Oh, the poor man!" Fraulein Lambeck put a hand on Anna's shoulder. "Are they doing everything for him? Does the doctor come to see him?"

"Yes," said Anna.

"And what does the doctor say?"

"He says . . . I don't know," said Anna.

Fraulein Lambeck leaned down confidentially and peered into her face. "Tell me, little Anna," she said, "how high is your dear Papa's temperature?"

"I don't know!" cried Anna, and her voice came out not at all as she had meant but in a sort of squeak. "I'm sorry but I must go home now!"—and she ran as fast as she could towards Max and the open front door.

"What's the matter with you?" said Heimpi in the hall. "Someone shoot you out of a cannon?"

Anna could see Mama through the half-open door in the drawing room.

"Mama!" she cried, "I hate lying to everybody about Papa. It's horrible. Why do we have to do it? I wish we didn't have to!"

Then she saw that Mama was not alone. Onkel Julius (who was not really an uncle but an old friend of Papa's) was sitting in an armchair on the other side of the room.

"Calm yourself," said Mama quite sharply. "We all hate lying about Papa, but just now it's necessary. I wouldn't ask you to do it if it weren't necessary!"

"She got caught by Fraulein Lambeck," said Max who had followed Anna in. "You know Fraulein Lambeck? She's ghastly. You can't answer her questions even when you're allowed to tell the truth!"

"Poor Anna," said Onkel Julius in his high voice. He was a gentle wispy man and they were all very fond of him. "Your father asked me to tell you that he misses you both very much and sends you lots of love."

"Have you seen him then?" asked Anna.

"Onkel Julius has just come back from Prague," said Mama. "Papa is fine, and he wants us to meet him in Zurich, in Switzerland, on Sunday."

"Sunday?" said Max. "But that's only a week. That's the

24

day of the elections. I thought we were going to wait and see who won, first!"

"Your father has decided he'd rather not wait." Onkel Julius smiled at Mama. "I do think he's taking all this too seriously."

"Why?" asked Max. "What's he worried about?"

Mama sighed. "Ever since Papa heard of the move to take away his passport he's been worried that they might try to take away ours—then we wouldn't be able to leave Germany."

"But why should they?" asked Max. "If the Nazis don't like us, surely they'd be glad to get rid of us."

"Exactly," said Onkel Julius. He smiled at Mama again. "Your husband is a wonderful man with a wonderful imagination, but frankly in this matter I think he's off his head. Never mind, you'll all have a lovely holiday in Switzerland and when you come back to Berlin in a few weeks time we'll all go to the Zoo together." Onkel Julius was a naturalist and went to the Zoo all the time. "Let me know if I can help with any of the arrangements. I'll see you again, of course." He kissed Mama's hand and went.

"Are we really leaving on Sunday?" asked Anna.

"Saturday," said Mama. "It's a long way to Switzerland. We have to spend a night in Stuttgart on the way."

"Then this is our last week at school!" said Max.

It seemed incredible.

Chapter Three

After that everything seemed to go very quickly, like a film that has been speeded up. Heimpi was busy sorting and packing all day long. Mama was nearly always out or on the telephone, arranging for the lease of the house or for the storage of the furniture after they had gone. Every day when the children came home from school the house looked more bare.

One day Onkel Julius called while they were helping Mama to pack some books. He looked at the empty shelves and smiled. "You'll be putting them all back again, you know!"

That night the children were woken up by the sound of fire engines. Not just one or two but about a dozen were clanging their bells and racing along the main road at the end of their street. When they looked out of the window the sky above the centre of Berlin was brilliant orange. Next morning everyone was talking about the fire which had destroyed the Reichstag where the German Parliament met. The Nazis said that the fire had been started by revolutionaries and that the

Nazis were the only people who could put a stop to that sort of thing—so everyone must vote for them at the elections. But Mama heard that the Nazis had started the fire themselves.

When Onkel Julius called that afternoon, for the first time he did not say anything to Mama about her being back in Berlin in a few weeks' time.

The last days Anna and Max spent at school were very strange. As they still were not allowed to tell anyone that they were leaving they kept forgetting about it themselves during school hours. Anna was delighted when she was given a part in the school play and only remembered afterwards that she would never actually appear in it. Max accepted an invitation to a birthday party which he would never be able to attend.

Then they would go home to the ever emptier rooms, the wooden crates and the suitcases, the endless sorting of possessions. Deciding which toys to take was the hardest part. They naturally wanted to take the games compendium but it was too big. In the end there was only room for some books and one of Anna's stuffed toys. Should she choose Pink Rabbit which had been her companion ever since she could remember or a newly acquired woolly dog? It seemed a pity to leave the dog when she had hardly had time to play with it, and Heimpi packed it for her. Max took his football. They could always have more things sent on to them in Switzerland, said Mama, if it looked as though they were going to stay there a very long time.

When school was over on Friday Anna went up to her teacher and said quietly, "I shan't be coming to school tomorrow. We're going to Switzerland."

Fraulein Schmidt did not look nearly as surprised as Anna expected but only nodded and said, "Yes . . . yes . . . I wish you luck."

Elsbeth was not very interested either. She just said she wished she herself were going to Switzerland but that this was not likely to happen because her father worked in the Post Office.

Gunther was the hardest person to leave. Max brought him

27

back to lunch after they had walked back from school together for the last time, though there were only sandwiches because Heimpi had not had time to cook. Afterwards they played hide-and-seek rather half-heartedly among the packing cases. It was not much fun because Max and Gunther were so gloomy, and Anna had a struggle to keep down her own excitement. She was fond of Gunther and sorry to leave him. But all she could think was, "This time tomorrow we'll be on the train . . . this time on Sunday we'll be in Switzerland . . . this time on Monday . . .?"

At last Gunther went home. Heimpi had sorted out a lot of clothes for his mum in the course of her packing and Max went with him to help him carry them. When he came back he seemed more cheerful. He had dreaded saying good-bye to Gunther more than anything. Now at least it was over.

Next morning Anna and Max were ready long before it was time to leave. Heimpi checked that their nails were clean, that they both had handkerchiefs—two for Anna because she had a bit of a cold—and that their socks were held up properly by elastic bands.

"Goodness knows what state you'll get into by yourselves," she grumbled.

"But you'll be with us again in a fortnight," said Anna.

"There's a lot of dirt can settle on a neck in a fortnight," said Heimpi darkly.

Then there was nothing more to do until the taxi came.

"Let's go right through the house for the last time," said Max.

They started at the top and worked down. Most of it no longer looked like itself. All the smaller things had been packed: Some of the rugs had been rolled up and there were newspapers and packing cases everywhere. They ticked off the rooms as they went through them, shouting "Good-bye Papa's bedroom . . . good-bye landing . . . good-bye stairs . . . !"

"Don't get too excited," said Mama as they passed her.

"Good-bye hall . . . good-bye drawing room . . . !"

They were getting through too quickly, so Max shouted, "Good-bye piano ... good-bye sofa ...!" and Anna took it up with, "Good-bye curtains ... good-bye dining table ... good-bye hatch...!"

Just as she shouted, "Good-bye hatch", its two small doors opened and Heimpi's head appeared looking through from the pantry. Suddenly something contracted in Anna's stomach. This was just what Heimpi had often done to amuse her when she was small. They had played a game called "peeping through the hatch" and Anna had loved it. How could she suddenly be going away? In spite of herself her eyes filled with tears and she cried, idiotically, "Oh Heimpi, I don't want to leave you and the hatch!"

"Well I can't pack it in my suitcase," said Heimpi, coming into the dining-room.

"You're sure you'll come to Switzerland?"

"I don't know what else I'd do," said Heimpi. "Your mama has given me my ticket and I've got it in my purse."

"Heimpi," said Max, "if you suddenly found you had a lot of room in your suitcase—only if, mind you—do you think you could bring the games compendium?"

"If ... if ... if ..." said Heimpi. "If my grandmother had wheels she'd be a bus and we could all go for a ride in her." That was what she always said.

Then the door-bell rang to announce the arrival of the taxi and there was no more time. Anna hugged Heimpi. Mama said, "Don't forget the men are coming for the piano on Monday", and then she too hugged Heimpi. Max could not find his gloves but had them in his pocket all the time. Bertha wept, and the man who looked after the garden suddenly appeared and wished them all a pleasant journey.

Just as the taxi was about to drive off a small figure rushed up with something in his hand. It was Gunther. He thrust a parcel at Max through the window and said something about his mum which they could not understand because the taxi had started. Max shouted good-bye and Gunther waved. Then the taxi went up the street. Anna could still see the house, and Heimpi and Gunther waving . . . She could still see a bit of the house . . . At the top of the street they passed the Kentner children on their way to school. They were talking to each other and did not look up . . . She could still see a tiny bit of the house through the trees . . . Then the taxi went round the corner and it all disappeared.

It was strange travelling on the train with Mama and without Heimpi. Anna was a little worried in case she felt sick. She had been train-sick a lot when she was small and even now that she had more or less outgrown it Heimpi always brought a paper bag just in case. Did Mama have a paper bag?

The train was crowded and Anna and Max were glad that they had window seats. They both looked out at the grey landscape tearing past until it began to rain. Then they watched the raindrops arrive with a splash and slowly trickle down the glass pane, but it became boring after a while. What now? Anna looked at Mama out of the corner of her eye. Heimpi usually had a few apples or some sweets about her.

Mama was leaning back in her seat. The corners of her mouth were pulled down and she was staring at the bald head of the man opposite without seeing him at all. On her lap was her big handbag with the picture of a camel on it which she had brought back from some journey with Papa. She was holding it very tight—Anna supposed because the tickets and passports were in it. She was clutching it so hard that one of her fingers was digging right in the camel's face.

"Mama," said Anna, "you're squashing the camel."

"What?" said Mama. Then she realised what Anna meant and loosened her hold on the bag. The camel's face reappeared, to Anna's relief, looking just as foolish and hopeful as usual.

"Are you bored?" asked Mama. "We'll be travelling right through Germany, which you have never done. I hope the rain stops soon so that you can see it all."

Then she told them about the orchards in Southern Germany —miles and miles of them. "If only we were making this

30

journey a little later in the year," she said, "you'd be able to see them all in blossom."

"Perhaps just a few of them might be out already," said Anna.

But Mama thought it was too early and the bald man agreed. Then they said how beautiful it was, and Anna wished she could see it.

"If the blossom isn't out this time," she said, "can we see it another time?"

Mama did not answer at once Then she said, "I hope so."

The rain did not let up and they spent a lot of time playing guessing games at which Mama turned out to be very good. Though they could not see much of the country they could hear the change in people's voices every time the train stopped. Some were almost incomprehensible and Max hit on the idea of asking unnecessary questions like "Is this Leipzig?" or "What time is it?" just for the pleasure of hearing the strangely accented replies.

They had lunch in the dining car. It was very grand with a menu to choose from and Anna had frankfurters and potato salad which was her favourite dish. She did not feel train-sick at all.

Later in the afternoon she and Max walked through the train from end to end and then stood in the corridor. The rain was heavier than ever and dusk came very early. Even if the orchards had been in blossom they would not have been able to see them. For a while they amused themselves by watching the fleeing darkness through their reflections on the glass. Then Anna's head began to ache and her nose began to run as though to keep pace with the rain outside. She snuggled back into her seat and wished they would get to Stuttgart.

"Why don't you look at Gunther's book?" said Mama.

There had been two presents in Gunther's parcel. One, from Gunther to Max, was a puzzle—a little transparent box with a picture of an open-mouthed monster drawn on the bottom. You had to get three tiny balls into the monster's mouth. It was very difficult to do on a train.

The other was a book for both children from Gunther's mum. It was called *They Grew To Be Great* and she had written in it, "Thank you for all the lovely things—something to read on the journey." It described the early lives of various people who later became famous, and Anna, who had a personal interest in the subject, leafed through it eagerly at first. But the book was so dully written and its tone was so determinedly uplifting that she gradually became discouraged.

All the famous people had had an awful time. One of them had a drunken father. Another had a stammer. Another had to wash hundreds of dirty bottles. They had all had what was called a difficult childhood. Clearly you had to have one if you wanted to become famous.

Dozing in her corner and mopping her nose with her two soaked handkerchiefs, Anna wished that they would get to Stuttgart and that one day, in the long-distant future, she might become famous. But as the train rumbled through Germany in the darkness she kept thinking "difficult childhood ... difficult childhood ... difficult childhood. ..."

Chapter Four

Suddenly she found herself being gently shaken. She must have been asleep. Mama said, "We'll be in Stuttgart in a few minutes."

Anna sleepily put on her coat, and soon she and Max were sitting on the luggage at the entrance of Stuttgart station while Mama went to get a taxi. The rain was still pelting down, drumming on the station roof and falling like a shiny curtain between them and the dark square in front of them. It was cold. At last Mama came back.

"What a place!" she cried. "They've got some sort of a strike on—something to do with the elections—and there are no taxis. But you see that blue sign over there?" On the opposite side of the square there was a bluish gleam among the wet. "That's a hotel," said Mama. "We'll just take what we need for the night and make a dash for it."

With the bulk of the luggage safely deposited they struggled across the ill-lit square. The case Anna was carrying kept banging against her leg and the rain was so heavy that she could hardly see. Once she missed her footing and stepped into a deep puddle so that her feet were soaked. But at last they were in the dry. Mama booked rooms for them and then she and Max had something to eat. Anna was too tired. She went straight to bed and to sleep.

In the morning they got up while it was still dark. "We'll soon see Papa," said Anna as they ate their breakfast in the dimly-lit dining-room. Nobody else was up yet and the sleepy-eyed waiter seemed to grudge them the stale rolls and coffee which he banged down in front of them. Mama waited until he had gone back into the kitchen. Then she said, "Before we get to Zurich and see Papa we have to cross the frontier between Germany and Switzerland."

"Do we have to get off the train?" asked Max.

"No," said Mama. "We just stay in our compartment and then a man will come and look at our passports—just like the ticket inspector. But"—and she looked at both children in turn— "this is very important. When the man comes to look at our passports I want neither of you to say anything. Do you understand? Not a word."

"Why not?" asked Anna.

"Because otherwise the man will say 'What a horrible talkative little girl, I think I'll take away her passport'," said Max who was always bad-tempered when he had not had enough sleep.

"Mama!" appealed Anna. "He wouldn't really—take away our passports, I mean?"

"No . . . no, I don't suppose so," said Mama. "But just in case—Papa's name is so well known—we don't want to draw attention to ourselves in any way. So when the man comes— not a word. Remember—not a single, solitary word!"

Anna promised to remember.

The rain had stopped at last and it was quite easy walking

back across the square to the station. The sky was just beginning to brighten and now Anna could see that there were election posters everywhere. Two or three people were standing outside a place marked Polling Station waiting for it to open. She wondered if they were going to vote and for whom.

The train was almost empty and they had a whole compartment to themselves until a lady with a basket got in at the next station. Anna could hear a sort of shuffling inside the basket—there must be something alive in it. She tried to catch Max's eye to see if he had heard it too, but he was still feeling cross and was frowning out of the window. Anna began to feel bad-tempered too and to remember that her head ached and that her boots were still wet from last night's rain.

"When do we get to the frontier?" she asked.

"I don't know," said Mama. "Not for a while yet." Anna noticed that her fingers were squashing the camel's face again.

"In about an hour, d'you think?" asked Anna.

"You never stop asking questions," said Max although it was none of his business. "Why can't you shut up?"

"Why can't you?" said Anna. She was bitterly hurt and cast around for something wounding to say. At last she came out with, "I wish I had a sister!"

"I wish I didn't!" said Max.

"Mama . . .!" wailed Anna.

"Oh, for goodness sake, stop it!" cried Mama. "Haven't we got enough to worry about?" She was clutching the camel bag and peering into it every so often to see if the passports were still there.

Anna wriggled crossly in her seat. Everybody was horrible. The lady with the basket had produced a large chunk of bread with some ham and was eating it. No one said anything for a long time. Then the train began to slow down.

"Excuse me," said Mama, "but are we coming to the Swiss frontier?"

The lady with the basket munched and shook her head.

"There, you see!" said Anna to Max. "Mama is asking questions too!"

Max did not even bother to answer but rolled his eyes up to heaven. Anna wanted to kick him, but Mama would have noticed.

The train stopped and started again, stopped and started again. Each time Mama asked if it was the frontier, and each time the lady with the basket shook her head. At last when the train slowed down yet again at the sight of a cluster of buildings, the lady with the basket said, "I daresay we're coming to it now."

They waited in silence while the train stood in the station. Anna could hear voices and the doors of other compartments opening and shutting. Then footsteps in the corridor. Then the door of their own compartment slid open and the passport inspector came in. He had a uniform rather like a ticket inspector and a large brown moustache.

He looked at the passport of the lady with the basket, nodded, stamped it with a little rubber stamp, and gave it back to her. Then he turned to Mama. Mama handed him the passports and smiled. But the hand with which she was holding her handbag was squeezing the camel into terrible contortions. The man examined the passports. Then he looked at Mama to see if it was the same face as on the passport photograph, then at Max and then at Anna. Then he got out his rubber stamp. Then he remembered something and looked at the passports again. Then at last he stamped them and gave them back to Mama.

"Pleasant journey," he said as he opened the door of the compartment.

Nothing had happened. Max had frightened her all for nothing.

"There, you see . . . !" cried Anna, but Mama gave her such a look that she stopped.

The passport inspector closed the door behind him.

"We are still in Germany," said Mama.

Anna could feel herself blushing scarlet. Mama put the passports back in the bag. There was a silence. Anna could hear whatever it was scuffling in the basket, the lady munching another piece of bread and ham, doors opening and shutting further and further along the train. It seemed to last for ever.

Then the train started, rolled a few hundred yards and stopped again. More opening and shutting of doors, this time more quickly. Voices saying, "Customs . . . anything to declare . . . ?" A different man came into the compartment. Mama and the lady both said they had nothing to declare and he made a mark with chalk on all their luggage, even on the lady's basket. Another wait, then a whistle and at last they started again. This time the train gathered speed and went on chugging steadily through the countryside.

After a long time Anna asked, "Are we in Switzerland yet?"

"I think so. I'm not sure," said Mama.

The lady with the basket stopped chewing. "Oh yes," she said comfortably, "this is Switzerland. We're in Switzerland now—this is my country."

It was marvellous.

"Switzerland!" said Anna. "We're really in Switzerland!"

"About time too!" said Max and grinned.

Mama put the camel bag down on the seat beside her and smiled and smiled.

"Well!" she said. "Well! We'll soon be with Papa."

Anna suddenly felt quite silly and light-headed. She wanted to do or say something extraordinary and exciting but could think of nothing at all—so she turned to the Swiss lady and said, "Excuse me, but what have you got in that basket?"

"That's my mogger," said the lady in her soft country voice.

For some reason this was terribly funny. Anna, biting back her laughter, glanced at Max and found that he too was almost in convulsions.

"What's a . . . what's a mogger?" she asked as the lady folded back the lid of the basket, and before anyone could answer there was a screech of "Meeee", and the head of a scruffy black tomcat appeared out of the opening.

At this Anna and Max could contain themselves no longer. They fell about with laughter.

"He answered you!" gasped Max. "You said, 'What's a mogger' and he said . . .'"

"Meeee!" screamed Anna.

"Children, children!" said Mama, but it was no good—they could not stop laughing. They laughed at everything they saw, all the way to Zurich. Mama apologised to the lady but she said she did not mind—she knew high spirits when she saw them. Any time they looked like flagging Max only had to say, "What's a mogger?" and Anna cried, "Meeee!" and they were off all over again. They were still laughing on the platform in Zurich when they were looking for Papa.

Anna saw him first. He was standing by a bookstall. His face was white and his eyes were searching the crowds milling round the train.

"Papa!" she shouted. "Papa!"

He turned and saw them. And then Papa, who was always so dignified, who never did anything in a hurry, suddenly ran towards them. He put his arms round Mama and hugged her. Then he hugged Anna and Max. He hugged and hugged them all and would not let them go.

"I couldn't see you," said Papa. "I was afraid . . ."

"I know," said Mama.

Chapter Five

Papa had reserved rooms for them in the best hotel in Zurich. It had a revolving door and thick carpets and lots of gold everywhere. As it was still only ten o'clock in the morning they ate another breakfast while they talked about everything that had happened since Papa had left Berlin.

At first there seemed endless things to tell him, but after a while they found it was nice just being together without saying anything at all. While Anna and Max ate their way through two different kinds of croissants and four different kinds of jam, Mama and Papa sat smiling at each other. Every so often they would remember something and Papa would say, "Did you manage to bring the books?" or Mama would say, "The paper rang and they'd like an article from you this week if possible." But then they would relapse back into their contented, smiling silence.

At last Max drank the last of his hot chocolate, wiped the last crumbs of croissant off his lips and said, "What shall we do now?"

Somehow nobody had thought.

After a moment Papa said, "Let's go and look at Zurich."

They decided first of all to go to the top of a hill overlooking the city. The hill was so steep that you had to go by funicular—a kind of lift on wheels that went straight up at an alarming angle. Anna had never been in one before and spent her time between excitement at the experience and anxious scrutiny of the cable for signs of fraying. From the top of the hill you could see Zurich clustered below at one end of an enormous blue lake. It was so big that the town seemed quite small by comparison, and its far end was hidden by mountains. Steamers, which looked like toys from this height, were making their way round the edge of the lake, stopping at each of the villages scattered along the shores and then moving on to the next. The sun was shining and made it all look very inviting.

"Can anyone go on those steamers?" asked Max. It was just what Anna had been going to ask.

"Would you like to go?" said Papa. "So you shall—this afternoon."

Lunch was splendid at a restaurant with a glassed-in terrace overlooking the lake below, but Anna could not eat much. Her head was feeling swimmy, probably from getting up so early, she thought, and though her nose had stopped running her throat was sore.

"Are you all right?" asked Mama anxiously.

"Oh yes!" said Anna, thinking of the steamer trip in the afternoon. Anyway, she was sure it was just tiredness.

There was a shop selling picture postcards next door to the restaurant and she bought one and sent it to Heimpi while Max sent one to Gunther.

"I wonder how they're getting on with the elections," said Mama. "Do you think the Germans will really vote for Hitler?"

"I'm afraid so," said Papa.

"They might not," said Max. "A lot of the boys at my

40

school were against him. We might find tomorrow that almost no one had voted for Hitler and then we could all go home again, just as Onkel Julius said."

"It's possible," said Papa, but Anna could see that he didn't really think so.

The steamer trip in the afternoon was a great success. Anna and Max stayed on the open deck in spite of the cold wind and watched the other traffic on the lake. Apart from the steamers there were private motor launches and even a few rowing boats. Their steamer went chug-chugging along from village to village on one side of the lake. These all looked very pretty, with their neat houses nestling among the woods and the hills. Whenever the steamer was getting near a landing stage it hooted loudly to let everyone in the village know that it was coming, and quite a lot of people got on and off each time. After about an hour it suddenly steamed straight across the lake to a village on the other side and then made its way back to Zurich where it had started.

As she walked back to the hotel through the noise of cars and buses and clanging trams Anna found she was very tired, and her head felt swimmy again. She was glad to get back to the hotel room which she shared with Max. She still was not hungry and Mama thought she looked so weary that she tucked her into bed straightaway. As soon as Anna put her head down on the pillow her whole bed seemed to take off and float away in the darkness with a chug-chugging noise which might have been a boat, or a train, or a sound coming from her own head.

Anna's first impression when she opened her eyes in the morning was that the room was far too bright. She closed them again quickly and lay quite still, trying to collect herself. There was a murmur of voices at the other end of the room and also a rustling sound which she could not identify. It must be quite late and everyone else must be up.

She opened her eyes again cautiously and this time the brightness heaved and swayed and finally rearranged itself into the room she knew, with Max, still in his pyjamas, sitting up in the other bed and Mama and Papa standing close by. Papa had a newspaper and this was what was making the rustling sound. They were talking quietly because they thought she was still asleep. Then the room gave another heave and she closed her eyes again and seemed to drift away somewhere while the voices went on.

Someone was saying ". . . so they've got a majority . . ." Then the voice faded away and another—(or was it the same one?)—said ". . . enough votes to do what he wants . . ." and then unmistakably Max, very unhappily, ". . . so we shan't be going back to Germany . . . so we shan't be going back to Germany . . . so we shan't be going back to Germany . . ." Had he really said it three times? Anna opened her eyes with a great effort and said "Mama!" At once one of the figures detached itself from the group and came towards her and suddenly Mama's face appeared quite close to hers. Anna said "Mama!" again and then all at once she was crying because her throat was so sore.

After this everything became vague. Mama and Papa were standing by her bed looking at a thermometer. Papa had his coat on. He must have gone out to buy the thermometer specially. Someone said, "A hundred and four," but it couldn't be her temperature they were talking about because she couldn't remember having it taken.

Next time she opened her eyes there was a man with a little beard looking at her. He said, "Well, young lady," and smiled and as he smiled his feet left the ground and he flew to the top of the wardrobe where he changed into a bird and sat croaking, "Influenza" until Mama shooed him out of the window.

Then suddenly it was night and she asked Max to get her some water, but Max was not there, it was Mama in the other bed. Anna said, "Why are you sleeping in Max's bed?" Mama said, "Because you're ill," and Anna felt very glad because if she was ill it meant that Heimpi would be coming to look after her. She said, "Tell Heimpi . . ." but then she was too tired to remember the rest, and the next time she looked the man with the little beard was there again and she didn't like him because he was upsetting Mama by saying, "Complications" over and over again. He had done something to the back of Anna's neck and had made it all swollen and sore, and now he was feeling it with his hand. She said, "Don't do that!" quite sharply, but he took no notice and tried to make her drink something horrible. Anna was going to push it away, but then she saw that it was not the man with the beard after all but Mama, and her blue eyes looked so fierce and determined that it didn't seem worth resisting.

After this the world grew a little steadier. She began to understand that she had been ill for some time, that she still had a high temperature and that the reason she felt so awful was that all the glands in her neck were enormously swollen and tender.

"We must get the temperature down," said the doctor with the beard.

Then Mama said, "I'm going to put something on your neck to make it better."

Anna saw some steam rising from a basin.

"It's too hot!" she cried. "I don't want it!"

"I won't put it on too hot," said Mama.

"I don't want it!" screamed Anna. "You don't know how to look after me! Where's Heimpi? Heimpi wouldn't put hot steam on my neck!"

"Nonsense!" said Mama, and suddenly she was holding a steaming pad of cotton wool against her own neck. "There," she said, "if it's not to hot for me it won't be too hot for you"— and she clapped it firmly on Anna's neck and quickly wrapped a bandage round it.

It was terribly hot but just bearable.

"That wasn't so bad, was it?" said Mama.

Anna was much too angry to answer and the room was beginning to spin again, but as she drifted off into vagueness she could just hear Mama's voice: "I'm going to get that temperature down if it kills me!"

43

After this she must have dozed or dreamed because suddenly her neck was quite cool again and Mama was unwrapping it.

"And how are you, fat pig?" said Mama.

"Fat pig?" said Anna weakly.

Mama very gently touched one of Anna's swollen glands.

"This is fat pig," she said. "It's the worst of the lot. The one next to it isn't quite so bad—it's called slim pig. And this one is called pink pig and this is baby pig and this one . . . what shall we call this one?"

"Fraulein Lambeck," said Anna and began to laugh. She was so weak that the laugh sounded more like a cackle but Mama seemed very pleased just the same.

Mama kept putting on the hot fomentations and it was not too bad because she always made jokes about fat pig and slim pig and Fraulein Lambeck, but though her neck felt better Anna's temperature still stayed up. She would wake up feeling fairly normal but by lunch time she would be giddy and by the evening everything would have become vague and confused. She got the strangest ideas. She was frightened of the wallpaper and could not bear to be alone. Once when Mama left her to go downstairs for supper she thought the room was getting smaller and smaller and cried because she thought she would be squashed. After this Mama had her supper on a tray in Anna's room. The doctor said, "She can't go on like this much longer."

Then one afternoon Anna was lying staring at the curtains. Mama had just drawn them because it was getting dark and Anna was trying to see what shapes the folds had made. The previous evening they had made a shape like an ostrich, and as Anna's temperature went up she had been able to see the ostrich more and more clearly until at last she had been able to make him walk all round the room. This time she thought perhaps there might be an elephant.

Suddenly she became aware of whispering at the other end of the room. She turned her head with difficulty. Papa was there, sitting with Mama, and they were looking at a letter together. She could not hear what Mama was saying, but she

44

could tell from the sound of her voice that she was excited and upset. Then Papa folded the letter and put his hand on Mama's, and Anna thought he would probably go soon but he didn't— he just stayed sitting there and holding Mama's hand. Anna watched them for a while until her eyes became tired and she closed them. The whispering voices had become more quiet and even. Somehow it was a very soothing sound and after a while Anna fell asleep listening to it.

When she woke up she knew at once that she had slept for a long time. There was something else, too, that was strange, but she could not quite make out what it was. The room was dim except for a light on the table by which Mama usually sat, and Anna thought she must have forgotten to switch it off when she went to bed. But Mama had not gone to bed. She was still sitting there with Papa just as they had done before Anna went to sleep. Papa was still holding Mama's hand in one of his and the folded letter in the other.

"Hullo Mama. Hullo Papa," said Anna. "I feel so peculiar."

Mama and Papa came over to her bed at once and Mama put a hand on her forehead. Then she popped the thermometer in Anna's mouth. When she took it out again she did not seem to be able to believe what she saw. "It's normal!" she said. "For the first time in four weeks it's normal!"

"Nothing else matters," said Papa and crumpled up the letter.

After this Anna got better quite quickly. Fat pig, slim pig, Fraulein Lambeck and the rest gradually shrank and her neck stopped hurting. She began to eat again and to read. Max came and played cards with her when he wasn't out somewhere with Papa, and soon she was allowed to get out of bed for a little while and sit in a chair. Mama had to help her walk the few steps across the room but she felt very happy sitting in the warm sunshine by the window.

Outside the sky was blue and she saw that the people in the street below were not wearing overcoats. There was a lady selling tulips at a stall on the opposite pavement and a chestnut tree at the corner was in full leaf. It was spring. She was amazed how much everything had changed during her illness. The people in the street seemed pleased with the spring weather too and several bought flowers from the stall. The lady selling tulips was round and dark-haired and looked a little bit like Heimpi.

Suddenly Anna remembered something. Heimpi had been going to join them two weeks after they left Germany. Now it must be more than a month. Why hadn't she come? She was going to ask Mama, but Max came in first.

"Max," said Anna, "why hasn't Heimpi come?"

Max looked taken aback. "Do you want to go back to bed?" he said.

"No," said Anna.

"Well," said Max, "I don't know if I'm meant to tell you, but quite a lot happened while you were ill."

"What?" asked Anna.

"You know Hitler won the elections," said Max. "Well he very quickly took over the whole government, and it's just as Papa said it would be—nobody's allowed to say a word against him. If they do they're thrown into jail."

"Did Heimpi say anything against Hitler?" asked Anna with a vision of Heimpi in a dungeon.

"No, of course not," said Max. "But Papa did. He still does. And so of course no one in Germany is allowed to print anything he writes. So he can't earn any money and we can't afford to pay Heimpi any wages."

"I see," said Anna, and after a moment she added, "are we poor, then?"

"I think we are, a bit," said Max. "Only Papa is going to try to write for some Swiss papers instead—then we'll be all right again." He got up as though to go and Anna said quickly, "I wouldn't have thought Heimpi would mind about money. If we had a little house I think she'd want to come and look after us anyway, even if we couldn't pay her much."

"Yes, well, that's another thing," said Max. He hesitated before he added, "We can't get a house because we haven't any furniture."

"But . . ." said Anna.

"The Nazis have pinched the lot," said Max. "It's called confiscation of property. Papa had a letter last week." He grinned. "It's been rather like one of those awful plays where people keep rushing in with bad news. And on top of it all there were you, just about to kick the bucket . . ."

"I wasn't going to kick the bucket!" said Anna indignantly.

"Well, I knew you weren't of course," said Max, "but that Swiss doctor has a very gloomy imagination. Do you want to go back to bed now?"

"I think I do," said Anna. She was feeling rather weak and Max helped her across the room. When she was safely back in bed she said, "Max, this . . . confiscation of property, whatever it's called—did the Nazis take everything—even our things?"

Max nodded.

Anna tried to imagine it. The piano was gone . . . the dining-room curtains with the flowers . . . her bed . . . all her toys which included her stuffed Pink Rabbit. For a moment she felt terribly sad about Pink Rabbit. It had had embroidered black eyes—the original glass ones had fallen out years before—and an endearing habit of collapsing on its paws. Its fur, though no longer very pink, had been soft and familiar. How could she ever have chosen to pack that characterless woolly dog in its stead? It had been a terrible mistake, and now she would never be able to put it right.

"I always knew we should have brought the games compendium," said Max. "Hitler's probably playing Snakes and Ladders with it this very minute."

"And snuggling my Pink Rabbit!" said Anna and laughed. But some tears had come into her eyes and were running down her cheeks all at the same time.

"Oh well, we're lucky to be here at all," said Max.

"What do you mean?" asked Anna.

Max looked carefully past her out of the window.

"Papa heard from Heimpi," he said with elaborate casualness. "The Nazis came for all our passports the morning after the elections."

47

Chapter Six

As soon as Anna was strong enough they moved out of their expensive hotel. Papa and Max had found an inn in one of the villages on the lake. It was called Gasthof Zwirn, after Herr Zwirn who owned it, and stood very near the landing stage, with a cobbled courtyard and a garden running down to the lake. People mostly came there to eat and drink, but Herr Zwirn also had a few rooms to let, and these were very cheap. Mama and Papa shared one room and Anna and Max another, so that it would be cheaper still.

Downstairs there was a large comfortable dining-room decorated with deers' antlers and bits of edelweiss. But when the weather became warmer tables and chairs appeared in the garden, and Frau Zwirn served everybody's meals under the chestnut trees overlooking the water. Anna thought it was lovely.

At weekends musicians came from the village and often played till late at night. You could listen to the music and watch the sparkle of the water through the leaves and the steamers gliding past. At dusk Herr Zwirn pressed a switch and little lights came on in the trees so that you could still see what you were eating. The steamers lit coloured lanterns to make themselves visible to other craft. Some were amber, but the prettiest were a deep, brilliant purply blue. Whenever Anna saw one of these magical blue lights against the darker blue sky and more dimly reflected in the dark lake, she felt as though she had been given a small present.

The Zwirns had three children who ran about barefoot and as Anna's legs began to feel less like cotton wool, she and Max went with them to explore the country round about. There were woods and streams and waterfalls, roads lined with apple trees and wild flowers everywhere. Sometimes Mama came with them rather than stay alone at the inn. Papa went to Zurich almost every day to talk to the editors of Swiss newspapers.

The Zwirn children, like everyone else living in the village, spoke a Swiss dialect which Anna and Max first found hard to understand. But they soon learned and the eldest, Franz, was able to teach Max to fish—only Max never caught anything—while his sister Vreneli showed Anna the local version of hopscotch.

In this pleasant atmosphere Anna soon recovered her strength and one day Mama announced that it was time for her and Max to start school again. Max would go to the Boys' High School in Zurich. He would travel by train, which was not as nice as the steamer but much quicker. Anna would go to the village school with the Zwirn children, and as she and Vreneli were roughly the same age they would be in the same class.

"You will be my best friend," said Vreneli. She had very long, very thin, mouse-coloured plaits and a worried expression.

Anna was not absolutely sure that she wanted to be Vreneli's best friend but thought it would be ungrateful to say so.

On Monday morning they set off together, Vreneli barefoot and carrying her shoes in her hand. As they approached the school they met other children, most of them also carrying their shoes. Vreneli introduced Anna to some of the girls, but the boys stayed on the other side of the road and stared across at them without speaking. Soon after they had reached the school playground a teacher rang a bell and there was a mad scramble by everyone to put their shoes on. It was a school rule that shoes must be worn but most children left them off till the last possible minute.

Anna's teacher was called Herr Graupe. He was quite old with a greyish yellowish beard, and everyone was much in awe of him. He assigned Anna a place next to a cheerful fair-haired girl called Roesli, and as Anna walked down the centre aisle of the classroom to her desk there was a general gasp.

"What's the matter?" Anna whispered as soon as Herr Graupe's back was turned.

"You walked down the centre aisle," Roesli whispered back. "Only the boys walk down the centre aisle."

"Where do the girls go?"

"Round the sides."

It seemed a strange arrangement, but Herr Graupe had begun to chalk up sums on the blackboard, so there was no time to go into it. The sums were very easy and Anna got them done quickly. Then she took a look round the classroom.

The boys were all sitting in two rows on one side, the girls on the other. It was quite different from the school she had gone to in Berlin where they had all been mixed up. When Herr Graupe called for the books to be handed in Vreneli got up to collect the girls' while a big red-haired boy collected the boys'. The red-haired boy walked up the middle of the classroom while Vreneli walked round the side until they met, each with a pile of books, in front of Herr Graupe's desk. Even there they were careful not to look at each other, but Anna noticed that Vreneli had turned a very faint shade of pink under her mouse-coloured hair.

At break-time the boys played football and horsed about on one side of the playground while the girls played hopscotch or sat sedately gossiping on the other. But though the girls pretended to take no notice of the boys they spent a lot of time watching them under their carefully lowered lids, and when Vreneli and Anna walked home for lunch Vreneli became so interested in the antics of the red-haired boy on the opposite side of the road that she nearly walked into a tree. They went back for an hour's singing in the afternoon and then school was finished for the day.

"How do you like it?" Mama asked Anna when she got back at three o'clock.

"It's very interesting," said Anna. "But it's funny—the boys and girls don't even talk to each other and I don't know if I'm going to learn very much."

When Herr Graupe had corrected the sums he had made several mistakes and his spelling had not been too good either.

"Well, it doesn't matter if you don't," said Mama. "It won't hurt you to have a bit of a rest after your illness."

"I like the singing," said Anna. "They can all yodel and they're going to teach me how to do it too."

"God forbid!" said Mama and immediately dropped a stitch.

Mama was learning to knit. She had never done it before, but Anna needed a new sweater and Mama was trying to save money. She had bought some wool and some knitting needles and Frau Zwirn had shown her how to use them. But somehow Mama never looked quite right doing it. Where Frau Zwirn sat clicking the needles lightly with her fingers, Mama knitted straight from the shoulder. Each time she pushed the needle into the wool it was like an attack. Each time she brought it out she pulled the stitch so tight that it almost broke. As a result the sweater only grew slowly and looked more like heavy tweed than knitting.

"I've never seen work quite like it," said Frau Zwirn,

astonished, when she saw it, "but it'll be lovely and warm when it's done."

One Sunday morning soon after Anna and Max had started school they saw a familiar figure get off the steamer and walk up the landing stage. It was Onkel Julius. He looked thinner than Anna remembered and it was wonderful and yet somehow confusing to see him—as though a bit of their house in Berlin had suddenly appeared by the edge of the lake.

"Julius!" cried Papa in delight when he saw him. "What on earth are you doing here?"

Onkel Julius gave a little wry smile and said, "Well, officially I'm not here at all. Do you know that nowadays it is considered very unwise even to visit you?" He had been to a naturalists' congress in Italy and had left a day early in order to come and see them on his way back to Berlin.

"I'm honoured and grateful," said Papa.

"The Nazis certainly are very stupid," said Onkel Julius. "How could you possibly be an enemy of Germany? You know of course that they burned all your books."

"I was in very good company," said Papa.

"What books?" asked Anna. "I thought the Nazis had just taken all our things—I didn't know they'd burned them."

"These were not the books your father owned," said Onkel Julius. "They were the books he has written. The Nazis lit big bonfires all over the country and threw on all the copies they could find and burned them."

"Along with the works of various other distinguished authors," said Papa, "such as Einstein, Freud, H. G. Wells..."

Onkel Julius shook his head at the madness of it all.

"Thank heavens you didn't take my advice," he said. "Thank heavens you left when you did. But of course," he added, "this situation in Germany can't go on much longer!"

Over lunch in the garden he told them the news. Heimpi had found a job with another family. It had been difficult because when people heard that she had worked for Papa they did not want to employ her. But it was not a bad job considering. Their house was still empty. Nobody had bought it yet.

It was strange, thought Anna, that Onkel Julius could go and look at it any time he liked. He could walk down the street from the paper shop at the corner and stand outside the white painted gate. The shutters would be closed but if he had a key Onkel Julius would be able to go through the front door into the dark hall, up the stairs to the nursery, or across into the drawing room, or along the passage to Heimpi's pantry ... Anna remembered it all so clearly, and in her mind she walked right through the house from top to bottom while Onkel Julius went on talking to Mama and Papa.

"How are things with you?" he asked. "Are you able to write here?"

Papa raised an eyebrow. "I have no difficulty in writing," he said, "only in getting my work published."

"Impossible!" said Onkel Julius.

"Unfortunately not," said Papa. "It seems the Swiss are so anxious to protect their neutrality that they are frightened of publishing anything by an avowed anti-Nazi like myself."

Onkel Julius looked shocked.

"Are you all right?" he asked. "I mean—financially?"

"We manage," said Papa. "Anyway, I'm trying to make them change their mind."

Then they began to talk about mutual friends. It sounded as though they were going through a long list of names. Somebody had been arrested by the Nazis. Somebody else had escaped and was going to America. Another person had compromised (what was "compromised" wondered Anna) and had written an article in praise of the new regime. The list went on and on. All grown-up conversations were like this nowadays, thought Anna, while little waves lapped against the edge of the lake and bees buzzed in the chestnut trees.

In the afternoon they showed Onkel Julius round. Anna and Max took him up into the woods and he was very interested to discover a special kind of toad that he had never seen before. Later they all went for a row on the lake in a hired boat.

53

Then they had supper together, and at last it was time for Onkel Julius to leave.

"I miss our outings to the Zoo," he said as he kissed Anna.

"So do I!" said Anna. "I liked the monkeys best."

"I'll send you a picture of one," said Onkel Julius.

They walked down to the landing stage together.

While they were waiting for the steamer Papa suddenly said, "Julius—don't go back. Stay here with us. You won't be safe in Germany."

"What—me?" said Onkel Julius in his high voice. "Who's going to bother about me? I'm only interested in animals. I'm not political. I'm not even Jewish unless you count my poor old grandmother!"

"Julius, you don't understand . . ." said Papa.

"The situation is bound to change," said Onkel Julius, and there was the steamer puffing towards them. "Good-bye old friend!" He embraced Papa and Mama and both children.

As he walked across the gangplank he turned back for a moment.

"Anyway," he said, "the monkeys at the Zoo would miss me!"

Chapter Seven

As Anna went on attending the village school she liked it more and more. She made friends with other girls apart from Vreneli, and especially with Roesli who sat next to her in class and was a little less sedate than the rest. The lessons were so easy that she was able to shine without any effort, and though Herr Graupe was not a very good teacher of the more conventional subjects he was a remarkable yodeller. Altogether what she liked best about the school was that it was so different from the one she had been to before She felt sorry for Max who seemed to be doing very much the same things at the Zurich High School as he had done in Berlin.

There was only one thing that bothered her. She missed playing with boys. In Berlin she and Max had mostly played with a mixed group of both boys and girls and it had been the same at school. Here the girls' endless hopscotch began to bore her and sometimes in break she looked longingly at the more exciting games and acrobatics of the boys.

One day there was no one even playing hopscotch. The boys were turning cartwheels and all the girls were sitting demurely watching them out of the corner of their eyes. Even Roesli who had cut her knee was sitting with the rest. Vreneli was particularly interested because the big red-haired boy was trying to turn cartwheels and the others were trying to teach him, but he kept flopping over sideways.

"Would you like to play hopscotch?" Anna asked her, but Vreneli shook her head, absorbed. It really was too silly, especially as Anna loved turning cartwheels herself—and it wasn't as though the red-haired boy was any good at it.

Suddenly she could stand it no longer and without thinking what she was doing she got up from her seat among the girls and walked over to the boys.

"Look," she said to the red-haired boy, "you've got to keep your legs straight like this"—and she turned a cartwheel to show him. All the other boys stopped turning cartwheels and stood back grinning. The red-haired boy hesitated.

"It's quite easy," said Anna. "You could do it if you'd only remember about your legs."

The red-haired boy still seemed undecided, but the other boys shouted, "Go on—try!" So he tried again and managed a little better. Anna showed him again, and this time he suddenly got the idea and turned a perfect cartwheel just as the bell went for the end of break.

Anna walked back to her own group and all the boys watched and grinned but the girls seemed mostly to be looking elsewhere. Vreneli looked frankly cross and only Roesli gave her a quick smile.

After break it was history and Herr Graupe decided to tell them about the cavemen. They had lived millions of years ago, he said. They killed wild animals and ate them and made their fur into clothes. Then they learned to light fires and make simple tools and gradually became civilised. This was progress, said Herr Graupe, and one way it was brought about was by pedlars who called at the cavemen's caves with useful objects for barter.

"What sort of useful objects?" asked one of the boys.

Herr Graupe peered indignantly over his beard. All sorts of things would be useful to cavemen, he said. Things like beads, and coloured wools, and safety-pins to fasten their furs together. Anna was very surprised to hear about the pedlars and the safety-pins. She longed to ask Herr Graupe whether he was really sure about them but thought perhaps it would be wiser not to. Anyway the bell went before she had the chance.

She was still thinking about the cavemen so much on the way home to lunch that she and Vreneli had walked nearly halfway before she realised that Vreneli was not speaking to her.

"What's the matter, Vreneli?" she asked.

Vreneli tossed her thin plaits and said nothing.

"What is it?" asked Anna again.

Vreneli would not look at her.

"You know!" she said. "You know perfectly well!"

"No, I don't," said Anna.

"You do!" said Vreneli.

"No, honestly I don't!" said Anna. "Please tell me."

But Vreneli wouldn't. She walked the rest of the way home without giving Anna a single glance, her nose in the air and her eyes fixed on some distant point. Only when they had reached the inn and were about to separate, did she look at her briefly, and Anna was surprised to see that she was not only angry but nearly in tears.

"Anyway," Vreneli shouted over her shoulder as she ran off, "anyway, we all saw your knickers!"

During lunch with Mama and Papa Anna was so quiet that Mama noticed it.

"Anything bother you at school?" she asked.

Anna considered. There were two things which had bothered her. One was Vreneli's extraordinary behaviour and the other was Herr Graupe's account of the cavemen. She decided

57

that the business about Vreneli was too complicated to explain and said instead, "Mama, did the cavemen really pin their furs together with safety-pins?" This produced such a flood of laughter, questions and explanations that they lasted until the end of lunch, and then it was time to go back to school. Vreneli had already left and Anna, feeling a little lonely, went on her own.

The afternoon lesson was singing again with a lot of yodelling which Anna enjoyed, and when it was over she suddenly found the red-haired boy standing in front of her.

"Hullo, Anna!" he said boldly. Some of his friends who were with him laughed, and before Anna could answer they had all turned on their heel and marched out of the classroom.

"Why did he say that?" asked Anna.

Roesli smiled. "I think you're going to have an escort," she said and added, "Poor Vreneli!"

Anna would have liked to ask her what she meant, but the mention of Vreneli reminded her that she must be quick if she did not want to walk home alone. So she said, "See you tomorrow," and ran.

There was no sign of Vreneli in the playground. Anna waited for a while, in case she might be in the cloakroom, but she did not appear. The only people in the playground were the red-haired boy and his friends, who also seemed to be waiting for someone. Vreneli must have rushed off early specially to avoid her. Anna went on hoping a little longer, but at last she had to admit to herself that it was no use and set off on her own. The red-haired boy and his friends decided to leave at exactly the same time.

It was less than ten minutes' walk back to the Gasthof Zwirn and Anna knew the way well. Outside the school gates she turned right and walked down the road. After a few moments she noticed that the red-haired boy and his friends had also turned right outside the school. The road led to a steep path covered in gravel which joined another road and this in turn, after some twists and turns, led to the inn.

It was while Anna was walking down the gravel path that

she first began to wonder whether everything was as it should be. The gravel was thick and very loose and her feet made a loud crunching sound at every step. Presently she became aware of similar, more muffled crunchings behind her. She listened to them for a few moments, then glanced over her shoulder. It was the red-haired boy and his friends again. Their shoes dangled from their hands and they were trudging through the gravel in their bare feet, apparently untroubled by the sharpness of the stones. Even Anna's brief glance had been enough to show her that they were all watching her.

She walked more quickly and the steps behind her quickened also. Then a little stone bounced off the gravel to one side of her. While she was still wondering where it had come from another little stone hit her leg. She turned round sharply and was just in time to see the red-haired boy pick up a bit of gravel and throw it at her.

"What are you doing?" she shouted. "Stop it!" But he just grinned and threw another bit. Then his friends began to throw some too. Most of it missed her and any stones that did hit her were too small to hurt, but it was horrid just the same.

Then she saw a small bandy-legged boy hardly bigger than herself pick up a whole handful of gravel.

"Don't you dare throw that at me!" she shouted so fiercely that the bandy-legged boy automatically took a step backwards. He threw the gravel in her direction but deliberately aimed short. Anna glared at him. The boys stood staring back at her.

Suddenly the red-haired boy took a step forward and shouted something. The others took it up in a sort of chant. "An-na! An-na!" they chanted. Then the red-haired boy threw another bit of gravel and hit her squarely on the shoulder. It was too much. She turned and fled.

Down the path, bits of gravel bouncing all round her, peppering her back, her legs. An-na! An-na! An-na! They were coming after her. Her feet slipped and slithered on the stones. If only she could get to the road at least they wouldn't be able to throw gravel at her. And there it was! Lovely smooth, hard asphalt under her feet. An-na! An-na! They were gaining ground. Now they were no longer stopping to pick up gravel they were coming on faster.

Suddenly a large object hurtled past her. A shoe! They were throwing their shoes at her! At least they'd have to stop to pick them up. She rounded a bend and could see the Gasthof Zwirn at the end of the road. The last bit was downhill and she almost threw herself down the slope as with one final effort she reached the courtyard of the inn.

An-na! An-na! Boys right behind her, shoes raining all round . . . And there, like a miracle, like an avenging angel, was Mama! She shot out of the inn like a torpedo. She grabbed the red-haired boy and slapped him. She hit another one with his own shoe. She flung herself into the group and scattered them. All the time she was shouting, "Why are you doing this? What's the matter with you?" That was what Anna wanted to know too.

Then she saw that Mama had got hold of the bandy-legged boy and was shaking him. All the rest had fled.

"Why did you chase her?" Mama was asking. "Why did you all throw things at her? What had she done?"

The bandy-legged boy scowled and wouldn't say.

"I won't let you go!" said Mama. "I won't let you go until you tell me why you did it!"

The bandy-legged boy looked hopelessly at Mama. Then he blushed and mumbled something.

"What?" said Mama.

Suddenly the bandy-legged boy grew desperate.

"Because we love her!" he shouted at the top of his voice. "We did it because we love her!"

Mama was so surprised that she let go of him and he shot away from her, across the courtyard and away down the road. "Because they love you?" said Mama to Anna. Neither of them could understand it. But when, later, they consulted Max he did not seem very surprised.

"It's what they do here," he said. "When they're in love with anyone they throw things at them."

"But, good heavens, there were six of them!" said Mama.

"Surely there must be other ways for them to express their love!"

Max shrugged. "It's what they do," he said and added, "Really Anna should feel honoured."

A few days later Anna saw him in the village, throwing unripe apples at Roesli.

Max was very adaptable.

Anna was not too sure about going back to school the next day. "Suppose they're still in love with me today?" she said. "I don't want to have more things thrown at me."

But she need not have worried. The boys had been so terrified by Mama that none of them dared as much as look at her. Even the red-haired boy kept his eyes carefully averted. So Vreneli forgave her and they were friends as before. Anna even managed to persuade her to try one cartwheel, secretly in a corner at the back of the inn. But in public, at school, they both stuck strictly to hopscotch.

Chapter Eight

On Anna's tenth birthday Papa was invited on an outing by the Zurich Literary Society, and when he mentioned Anna's birthday they invited her and Max and Mama as well. Mama was delighted.

"How lucky that it should just be on your birthday," she said. "What a lovely way to celebrate."

But Anna did not think so at all. She said, "Why can't I have a party as usual?" Mama looked taken aback.

"But it's not the same as usual," she said. "We're not at home."

Anna knew this really, but she still felt that her birthday ought to be something special for her—not just an outing in which everyone else was included. She said nothing.

"Look," said Mama, "it'll be lovely. They're going to hire a steamer, just for the people on the outing. We're going nearly to the other end of the lake and having a picnic on an island, and we won't be home till late!" But Anna was not convinced.

She did not feel any better when the day arrived and she saw her presents. There was a card from Onkel Julius, some crayons from Max, a small pencil box and a wooden chamois from Mama and Papa. That was all. The chamois was very pretty, but when Max was ten his birthday present had been a new bicycle. The card from Onkel Julius had a picture of a monkey on it and he had written on the back in his meticulous handwriting, "A happy birthday, and many more even happier ones to come." Anna hoped he was right about the birthdays to come, because this one certainly did not look very promising.

"It's a funny sort of birthday for you this year," said Mama, seeing her face. "Anyway you're really getting too big to bother much with presents." But she hadn't said that to Max when he was ten. And it wasn't as though it were just any birthday, thought Anna. It was her first birthday with double figures.

As the day wore on she felt worse and worse. The outing was not really a success. The weather was lovely but it became very hot on the steamer and the members of the literary society all talked like Fraulein Lambeck. One of them actually addressed Papa as "dear Master". He was a fat young man with lots of small sharp teeth, and he interrupted just as Anna and Papa were starting a conversation.

"I was so sorry about your article, dear Master," said the fat young man.

"I was sorry too," said Papa. "This is my daughter Anna who is ten today."

"Happy birthday," said the young man briefly and at once went back to talking to Papa. It was such a pity that he hadn't been able to print Papa's article, especially as it was so splendid. The young man had admired it enormously. But the dear Master had such strong opinions . . . the policy of the paper . . . the feelings of the government . . . the dear Master must understand . . .

"I understand entirely," said Papa, turning away, but the fat young man held on.

Such difficult times, said the young man. Fancy the Nazis burning Papa's books—Papa must have felt terrible. The young man knew just how terrible Papa must have felt because as it happened he had just had his own first book published and could imagine . . . Had the dear Master by any chance seen the young man's first book? No? Then the young man would tell him about it . . .

He talked and talked with his little teeth clicking away and Papa was too polite to stop him. At last Anna could stand it no longer and wandered off.

The picnic, too proved a disappointment. It consisted largely of bread rolls with rather grown-up fillings. The rolls were hard and a bit stale so that only the fat young man with the teeth, thought Anna, could have chewed his way through them. For drink there was ginger beer which she hated but Max liked. It was all right for him. He had brought his fishing rod and was quite content to sit on the edge of the island and fish. (Not that he caught anything—but then he was using bits of the stale rolls for bait and it was not surprising that the fish did not like them either.)

There was nothing for Anna to do. There were no other children to play with and after lunch it was even worse because there were speeches. Mama had not told her about the speeches. She should have warned her. They went on for what seemed like hours and Anna sat through them miserably in the heat, thinking of what she would have been doing if they had not had to leave Berlin.

Heimpi would have made a birthday cake with strawberries. She would have had a party with at least twenty children and each of them would have brought her a present. About now they would all be playing games in the garden. Then there would be tea, and candles round the cake . . . She could imagine it all so clearly that she hardly noticed when the speeches finally came to an end.

Mama appeared beside her. "We're going back to the boat now," she said. Then she whispered, "The speeches were dreadfully dull, weren't they?" with a conspiratorial smile. But Anna did not smile back. It was all very well for Mama—after all it wasn't her birthday!

Once back on the boat she found a place by the side and stood there alone, staring into the water. That was it, she thought as the boat steamed back towards Zurich. She'd had her birthday—her tenth birthday—and not a single bit of it had been nice. She folded her arms on the railings and rested her head on them, pretending to look at the view so that no one should see how miserable she was. The water rushed past below her and the warm wind blew through her hair, and all she could think of was that her birthday had been spoilt and nothing would ever be any good again.

After a while she felt a hand on her shoulder. It was Papa. Had he noticed how disappointed she was? But Papa never noticed things like that—he was too absorbed in his own thoughts.

"So now I have a ten-year-old daughter," he said and smiled.

"Yes," said Anna.

"As a matter of fact," said Papa, "I don't think you are quite ten years old yet. You were born at six o'clock in the evening. That's not for another twenty minutes."

"Really?" said Anna. For some reason the fact that she was not quite ten yet made her feel better.

"Yes," said Papa, "and to me it doesn't seem so very long ago. Of course we didn't know then that we'd be spending your tenth birthday steaming about Lake Zurich as refugees from Hitler."

"Is a refugee someone who's had to leave their home?" asked Anna.

"Someone who seeks refuge in another country," said Papa.

"I don't think I'm quite used to being one yet," said Anna.

"It's an odd feeling," said Papa. "You live in a country

all your life. Then suddenly it is taken over by thugs and there you are, on your own in a strange place, with nothing."

He looked so cheerful as he said this that Anna asked, "Don't you mind?"

"In a way," said Papa. "But I find it very interesting."

The sun was sinking in the sky. Every so often it disappeared behind the top of a mountain, and then the lake darkened and everything on the boat became dull and flat. Then it reappeared in a gap between two peaks and the world turned rosy-gold again.

"I wonder where we'll be on your eleventh birthday," said Papa, "and on your twelfth."

"Won't we be here?"

"Oh, I don't think so," said Papa. "If the Swiss won't print anything I write for fear of upsetting the Nazis across the border we may as well live in another country altogether. Where would you like to go?"

"I don't know," said Anna.

"I think France would be very nice," said Papa. He considered it for a while. "Do you know Paris at all?" he asked.

Until Anna became a refugee the only place she had ever gone to was the seaside, but she was used to Papa's habit of becoming so interested in his own thoughts that he forgot whom he was talking to. She shook her head.

"It's a beautiful city," said Papa. "I'm sure you'd like it."

"Would we go to a French school?"

"I expect so. And you'd learn to speak French. On the other hand," said Papa, "we might live in England—that's very beautiful too. But a bit damp." He looked at Anna thoughtfully. "No," he said, "I think we'll try Paris first."

The sun had now disappeared completely and it was dusk. It was hard to see the water as the boat sped through it, except for the foam which flashed white in what little light was left.

"Am I ten yet?" asked Anna. Papa looked at his watch.

"Ten years old exactly." He hugged her. "Happy, happy birthday, and very many happy returns!"

And just as he said it the boat's lights came on. There was

66

only a sprinkling of white bulbs round the rails which left the deck almost as dark as before, but the cabin suddenly glowed yellow and at the back of the boat the ship's lantern shone a brilliant purply-blue.

"Isn't it lovely!" cried Anna and somehow, suddenly, she no longer minded about her birthday and her presents. It seemed rather fine and adventurous to be a refugee, to have no home and not to know where one was going to live. Perhaps at a pinch it might even count as a difficult childhood like the ones in Gunther's book and she would end up by being famous.

As the boat steamed back to Zurich she snuggled up to Papa and they watched the blue light from the ship's lantern trailing through the dark water behind them.

"I think I might quite like being a refugee," said Anna.

Chapter Nine

The summer wore on and suddenly it was the end of term. On
the last day there was a celebration at school with a speech by
Herr Graupe, an exhibition of needlework by the girls, a gym
display by the boys and much singing and yodelling by everyone. At the end of the afternoon each child was presented with
a sausage and a hunk of bread, and they wandered home
through the village chewing and laughing and making plans
for the next day. The summer holidays had begun.

Max did not finish until a day or two later. At the High
School in Zurich the term did not end with yodelling and
sausages but with reports. Max brought home his usual quota
of comments like "Does not try" and "Shows no interest", and
he and Anna sat through the usual gloomy lunch while Mama

and Papa read them. Mama was particularly disappointed because, while she had got used to Max not trying and showing no interest in Germany, she had somehow hoped it might be different in Switzerland—because Max was clever, only he did not work. But the only difference was that whereas in Germany Max had neglected his work to play football, in Switzerland he neglected it in order to fish, and the results were much the same.

It was amazing, thought Anna, how he went on with his fishing even though he never caught anything. Even the Zwirn children had begun to tease him about it. "Bathing worms again?" they would say as they passed him and he would scowl at them furiously, unable to shout an insult back for fear of disturbing some fish that might just be going to bite.

When Max was not fishing he and Anna and the three Zwirn children swam in the lake and played together or went for walks in the woods. Max got on well with Franz, and Anna had become quite fond of Vreneli. Trudi was only six, but she trailed along behind no matter what the others were doing. Sometimes they were joined by Roesli and once even by the red-haired boy who studiously ignored both Anna and Vreneli and only talked about football to Max.

Then one morning Anna and Max came down to find the Zwirn children playing with a boy and a girl they had never seen before. They were German, about their own ages, and were spending a holiday with their parents at the inn.

"Which part of Germany do you come from?" asked Max.

"Munich," said the boy.

"We used to live in Berlin," said Anna.

"Gosh," said the boy, "Berlin must be marvellous."

They all played chase together. It had never been much fun before because there had only been four of them—(Trudi did not count because she could not run fast enough and always cried when anyone caught her). But the German children were both very quick on their feet and for the first time the game was really exciting. Vreneli had just caught the German boy, and he caught Anna, so now it was Anna's turn to catch someone and she chased after the German girl. They raced round and round the courtyard of the inn, doubling back and forth and leaping over things until Anna thought she was just going to catch her—but all at once her path was blocked by a tall thin lady with a disagreeable expression. The lady appeared so suddenly, apparently from nowhere, that Anna was barely able to stop and almost collided with her.

"Sorry," she said, but the lady did not reply.

"Siegfried!" she called shrilly. "Gudrun! I told you you were not to play with these children!" She grabbed hold of the German girl and pulled her away. The boy followed, but when his mother was not looking he made a funny face at Anna and waved his hands apologetically. Then the three of them disappeared into the inn.

"What a cross woman," said Vreneli.

"Perhaps she thinks we're badly brought up," said Anna.

They tried to go on playing chase without the German children, but it was no good and ended in the usual shambles, with Trudi in tears because she had been caught.

Anna did not see the German children again until the late afternoon. They must have been shopping in Zurich for they were each carrying a parcel and their mother had several large ones. As they were about to go into the inn Anna thought this was her chance to show that she was not badly brought up. She leapt forward and opened the door for them.

But the German lady did not seem at all pleased. "Gudrun! Siegfried!" she said and pushed her children quickly inside. Then, with a sour expression and keeping as far away from Anna as possible, she squeezed past herself. It was difficult because of the parcels which nearly stuck in the doorway, but at last she was through and disappeared. With never a word of thanks, thought Anna—the German lady was badly brought up herself!

The next day she and Max had arranged to go up into the woods with the Zwirn children, and the day after that it rained, and the day after that Mama took them to Zurich to buy them some socks—so they did not see the German children. But after breakfast on the following morning when Anna and Max went out into the yard, there they were again playing with the Zwirns. Anna rushed up to them.

"Shall we have a game of chase?" she said.

"No," said Vreneli, looking rather pink. "And any way you can't play."

Anna was so surprised that for a moment she could think of nothing to say. Was Vreneli upset about the red-haired boy again? But she hadn't seen him for ages.

"Why can't Anna play?" asked Max.

Franz was as embarrassed as his sister.

"Neither of you can," he said and indicated the German children. "They say they're not allowed to play with you."

The German children had clearly not only been forbidden to play but even to talk to them, for the boy looked as though he wanted to say something. But in the end he only made his funny apologetic face and shrugged.

Anna and Max looked at each other. They had never met such a situation before. Then Trudi who had been listening suddenly sang out, "Anna and Max can't play! Anna and Max can't play!"

"Oh, shut up!" said Franz. "Come on!" and he and Vreneli ran off towards the lake with the German children following. For a moment Trudi was taken aback. Then she sang out one last defiant "Anna and Max can't play!" and scampered after them on her short legs.

Anna and Max were left standing.

"Why aren't they allowed to play with us?" asked Anna, but Max didn't know either. There seemed nothing to do but wander back to the dining-room where Mama and Papa were still finishing breakfast.

"I thought you were playing with Franz and Vreneli," said Mama.

Max explained what had happened.

"That's very odd," said Mama.

"Perhaps you could speak to the mother," said Anna. She

71

had just noticed the German lady and a man who must be her husband sitting at a table in the corner.

"I certainly will," said Mama.

Just then the German lady and her husband got up to leave the dining-room and Mama went to intercept them. They met too far away for Anna to hear what they said, but Mama had only spoken a few words when the German lady answered something which caused Mama to flush with anger. The German lady said something more and made as though to move off. But Mama grabbed her arm.

"Oh no, it isn't!" shouted Mama in a voice which echoed right across the dining-room. "It's not the end of it at all!" Then she turned on her heel and marched back to the table while the German lady and her husband went out looking down their noses.

"The whole room could hear you," said Papa crossly as Mama sat down. He hated scenes.

"Good!" said Mama in such ringing tones that Papa whispered Ssssh! and made calming motions with his hands. Trying to speak quietly made Mama angrier than ever and she could hardly get the words out.

"They're Nazis," she said at last. "They've forbidden their children to play with ours because our children are Jewish!" Her voice rose higher in indignation. "And you want me to keep my voice down!" she shouted so that an old lady still finishing breakfast was startled into almost spilling her coffee.

Papa's mouth tightened. "I would not dream of allowing Anna and Max to play with the children of Nazis," he said, "so there is no difficulty."

"But what about Vreneli and Franz?" asked Max. "It means that if they're playing with the German children they can't play with us."

"I think Vreneli and Franz will have to decide who their friends are," said Papa. "Swiss neutrality is all very well, but it can be taken too far." He got up from the table. "I'll have a word with their father now."

A little while later Papa returned. He had told Herr Zwirn that his children must choose whether they wished to play with Anna and Max or with the German visitors. They could not play with both. Papa had asked them not to decide in a hurry but to let him know that evening.

"I suppose they'll choose us," said Max. "After all we'll be here long after those other children have gone."

But it was difficult to know what to do with the rest of the day. Max went down to the lake with his fishing rod and his worms and his bits of bread. Anna could not settle to anything. At last she decided to write a poem about an avalanche which engulfed an entire city, but it did not turn out very well. When she came to do the illustration she was so bored at the thought of making it all white that she gave up. Max, as usual, caught no fish and by mid-afternoon they were both so depressed that Mama gave them half a franc to buy themselves some chocolate —although she had previously said it was too expensive.

On their way back from the sweet-shop they caught a glimpse of Vreneli and Franz talking earnestly in the doorway of the inn and walked past self-consciously looking straight ahead. This made them feel worse than ever.

Then Max went back to his fishing and Anna decided to go for a bathe, to try and salvage something from the day. She floated on her back which she had only just learned to do, but it did not cheer her up. It all seemed so silly. Why couldn't she and Max and the Zwirns and the German children all play together? Why did they have to have all this business of decisions and taking sides?

Suddenly there was a splash in the water beside her. It was Vreneli. Her long thin plaits were tied in a knot on top of her head so as not to get wet and her long thin face looked pinker and more worried than ever.

"I'm sorry about this morning," said Vreneli breathlessly. "We've decided we'd rather play with you even if it does mean that we can't play with Siegfried and Gudrun."

Then Franz appeared on the bank. "Hullo, Max!" he shouted. "Worms enjoying their swim?"

73

"I'd have caught a great big fish just then," said Max, "if you hadn't frightened it away." But he was very pleased just the same.

At supper that evening Anna saw the German children for the last time. They were sitting stiffly in the dining-room with their parents. Their mother was talking to them quietly and insistently, and even the boy never turned round once to look at Anna or Max. At the end of the meal he walked right past their table as though he could not see them.

The whole family left the next morning.

"I'm afraid we've lost Herr Zwirn some customers," said Papa.

Mama was triumphant.

"But it seems such a pity," said Anna. "I'm sure that boy really liked us."

Max shook his head. "He didn't like us any more at the end," he said. "Not by the time his mother had finished with him."

It was true, thought Anna. She wondered what the German boy was thinking now, what his mother had told him about her and Max, and what he would be like when he grew up.

Chapter Ten

Just before the end of the summer holidays Papa went to Paris. There were so many German refugees living there now that they had started their own newspaper. It was called the *Daily Parisian* and some of the articles Papa had written in Zurich had appeared in it. Now the editor wanted him to write for the paper on a more regular basis. Papa thought that if it worked out they might all go to Paris to live.

The day after he left Omama arrived. She was the children's grandmother and had come on a visit from the South of France.

"How funny," said Anna. "Omama might pass Papa in the train. They could wave to each other!"

"They wouldn't, though," said Max. "They don't get on."

"Why not?" asked Anna. It was true, now she came to think of it, that Omama only came to see them when Papa was away.

"One of those family things," said Max in an irritating would-be grown-up voice. "She didn't want Mama and Papa to marry each other."

"Well, it's a bit late now!" said Anna with a giggle.

Anna was out playing with Vreneli when Omama arrived, but she knew at once that she had come because of the hysterical barking that issued from an open window of the inn. Omama never moved without her dachshund Pumpel. She followed the sound and found Omama with Mama.

"Darling Anna!" cried Omama. "How lovely to see you!" and she hugged Anna to her stout bosom. After a moment Anna thought the hug must be finished and wriggled, but Omama held on tight and hugged her a bit more. Anna remembered that Omama had always done this.

"It's been such a long time!" cried Omama. "That dreadful man Hitler . . .!" Her eyes, which were blue like Mama's but much paler, filled with tears and her chins—there were two—trembled gently. It was difficult to hear exactly what she was saying because of Pumpel's noise. Only a few phrases like "torn from our homes" and "breaking up families" emerged above the frantic barks.

"What's the matter with Pumpel?" asked Anna.

"Oh Pumpel, my poor Pumpel! Just look at him!" cried Omama.

Anna had been looking at him. He was behaving very strangely. His brown hindquarters stuck straight up into the air and he kept flattening his head on his front paws as though he were bowing. Between bows he gazed beseechingly at something above Omama's wash basin. Since Pumpel was the same tubby shape as Omama the whole operation was very difficult for him.

"What does he want?" asked Anna.

"He's begging," said Omama. "Isn't he sweet? He's begging for that electric light bulb. Oh, but Pumpel, my darling Pumpel, I can't give it to you!"

Anna looked. Above the basin was a perfectly ordinary round bulb, painted white. It seemed an eccentric thing even for Pumpel to wish for.

"Why does he want it?" she asked.

"Well, of course he doesn't realise it's a bulb," Omama explained patiently. "He thinks it's a tennis ball and he wants me to throw it for him."

Pumpel, sensing that his needs were at last being taken seriously, bowed and barked with redoubled vigour.

Anna laughed. "Poor Pumpel," she said and tried to stroke him—but he immediately snapped at her hand with his yellow teeth. She withdrew it quickly.

"We could unscrew the bulb," said Mama, but it was stuck fast in its socket and would not be moved.

"Perhaps if we had a real tennis ball . . ." said Omama, searching for her purse. "Anna darling, would you mind? I think the shops are still open."

"Tennis balls are quite expensive," said Anna. She had once wanted to buy one with her pocket money but had not had nearly enough.

"It doesn't matter," said Omama, "I can't leave poor Pumpel like this—he'll exhaust himself."

But when Anna returned Pumpel had lost interest in the whole business. He was lying on the floor growling, and when Anna placed the ball gingerly between his paws he gave it a look of utter loathing and sank his teeth straight into it. The tennis ball expired with a sigh. Pumpel got up, scratched the floor twice with his hind feet, and retired under the bed.

"He really is a horrible dog," Anna later told Max. "I don't know how Omama puts up with him."

"I wish we had the money for the tennis ball," said Max. "We could use it at the fair."

There was a fair coming to the village—an annual event which the local children were very excited about. Franz and Vreneli had been saving up their pocket money for months. Somehow Anna and Max had only just heard about it, and as they had no savings they did not see how they could go. Their combined assets would just about pay for one ride on the roundabout—and that, said Anna, would be worse than not going at all.

She had thought briefly of asking Mama for some money. This was after her first day back at school when no one had talked about anything except the fair and how much money they would have to spend. But Max had reminded her that Mama was trying to economise. If they were going to live in Paris they would need every penny for the move.

Meanwhile Pumpel, though no one could call him lovable, made life a lot more interesting. He had no sense at all. Even Omama who was used to his ways was surprised. When she took him on a steamer he made straight for the side and was only restrained with difficulty from throwing himself overboard. The next time she wanted to go to Zurich she tried to take him on the train, but he refused to get on it. However, as soon as the train pulled out of the station, leaving Omama and Pumpel on the platform, he tore himself free from his lead and pursued it, barking wildly, right down the line to the next village. He was brought back exhausted an hour later by a small boy and had to rest for the remainder of the day.

"Do you think there's something wrong with his eyesight?" asked Omama.

"Nonsense, Mother," said Mama who felt she had more important worries, what with possibly moving to Paris and having no money. "Anyway, even if there is you can't buy him spectacles!"

It was a shame because Omama, in spite of being silly about Pumpel, was really very kind. She too was a refugee but her husband was not famous like Papa. They had been able to move all their belongings out of Germany and now lived comfortably by the Mediterranean. Unlike Mama, she did not have to economise and often devised little treats which Mama would not normally have been able to afford.

"I suppose we couldn't ask Omama to give us some money for the fair?" said Anna one day after Omama had bought them all éclairs at the local cake shop.

Max was horrified. "Anna! We couldn't!" he said quite sharply.

Anna had known really that they couldn't—only it was so tempting. The fair was only about a week away.

A few days before Omama was due to travel back to the South of France, Pumpel disappeared. He had escaped from Omama's room early in the morning and she had thought nothing of it. He often went for a sniff round the lake and usually came back quite quickly of his own accord. But by breakfast time he was still missing and she began to ask people whether they had seen him.

"Whatever has he got up to now?" said Herr Zwirn. He did not like Pumpel who upset his other customers, chewed the furniture and had twice tried to bite Trudi.

"Sometimes he seems to act just like a puppy," said Omama fondly, though Pumpel was nine years old.

"It's more like his second childhood," said Herr Zwirn.

The children searched for him half-heartedly, but it was nearly time to go to school and they were sure that sooner or later he would turn up—probably accompanied by an angry victim whom he had either bitten or whose property he had destroyed. Vreneli came to call for Anna and they set off for school, and Anna promptly forgot all about him. When they returned at lunch-time they were met by Trudi with an air of great importance.

"They found your grandmother's dog," she said. "He's drownded."

"Nonsense!" said Vreneli. "You're making it up."

"I'm not making it up," said Trudi, outraged. "It's true—Pa found him in the lake. And I've seen him myself and he's quite dead. One reason I knew he was dead was because he didn't try to bite me."

Mama confirmed Trudi's story. Pumpel had been found at the bottom of a low wall at the edge of the lake. No one ever discovered how he got there—whether he had leapt down in a fit of madness or mistaken one of the large pebbles in the water for a tennis ball. Herr Zwirn suggested that it might have been suicide.

"I've heard of dogs doing that," he said, "when they're no good to themselves or to anyone else."

Poor Omama was dreadfully upset. She did not come down to lunch and only appeared, red-eyed and silent, for Pumpel's funeral in the afternoon. Herr Zwirn dug a little grave for him in a corner of the garden. Omama had wrapped Pumpel up in an old shawl and the children all stood by while she put him in his last resting place. Then, under Omama's direction, they each threw a shovelful of soil on top of him. Herr Zwirn briskly threw on a whole lot more and then flattened and shaped it into a low mound.

"Now for the decoration," said Herr Zwirn, and Omama tearfully placed a large plant-pot with a chrysanthemum on top.

Trudi watched her approvingly.

"Now your doggie can't get out!" she said with obvious satisfaction.

This was too much for Omama, and to the children's embarrassment she burst into tears and had to be led away by Herr Zwirn.

The rest of the day was rather gloomy. Nobody really minded about poor Pumpel except Omama, but they all felt they owed it to her not to look too cheerful. After supper Max went off to do his homework while Anna and Mama kept Omama company.

She had hardly said a word all day, but now she suddenly could not stop talking. On and on she went about Pumpel and all the things he used to do. How could she face travelling back to the South of France without him? He had been such good company on the train. She even had his return ticket— both Mama and Anna had to inspect it. It was all the fault of the Nazis, cried Omama. If Pumpel had not had to leave Germany he would never have drowned in Lake Zurich. That dreadful man Hitler . . .

After this Mama gradually turned the talk into the usual

list of people who had gone to live in different countries or had stayed behind and Anna began to read, but her book was not very interesting and bits of the conversation kept filtering through.

Somebody had got a job in films in England. Somebody else who had been rich was now very hard up in America and his wife had to go out cleaning. A famous professor had been arrested and sent to a concentration camp. (Concentration camp? Then Anna remembered that it was a special prison for people who were against Hitler.) The Nazis had chained him to a dog kennel. What a silly thing to do, thought Anna, as Omama, who seemed to see some connection between this and Pumpel's death, talked more and more excitedly. The dog kennel was right by the entrance to the concentration camp and every time anyone went in or out the famous professor had to bark. He was given scraps to eat out of a dog-dish and was not allowed to touch them with his hands.

Anna suddenly felt sick.

At night the famous professor had to sleep in the dog kennel. The chain was too short for him ever to stand up straight. After two months—two months . . .! thought Anna—the famous professor had gone mad. He was still chained to the dog kennel and having to bark but he no longer knew what he was doing.

A black wall seemed suddenly to have risen up in front of Anna's eyes. She could not breathe. She clutched her book in front of her, pretending to read. She wanted not to have heard what Omama had said, to be rid of it, to be sick.

Mama must have sensed something, for there was a sudden silence and Anna could feel Mama looking at her. She stared down fiercely at her book and deliberately turned a page as though absorbed. She did not want Mama and especially Omama to speak to her.

After a moment the conversation started up again. This time Mama was talking rather loudly not about concentration camps but about how cold it had been lately.

"Enjoying your book, dear?" said Omama.

"Yes, thank you," said Anna and managed to make her voice sound quite normal. As soon as possible she got up and went to bed. She wanted to tell Max what she had heard but could not bring herself to talk about it. It was better not even to think about it.

In future she would try never to think about Germany at all.

The next morning Omama packed her bags. She had no heart to stay the last few days, now that Pumpel was gone. But there was one good thing that came of her visit. Just before she left she handed Anna and Max an envelope. She had written on it, "A present from Pumpel" and when they opened it they found that it contained a little over eleven Swiss francs.

"I want you to use this money in any way that gives you pleasure," said Omama.

"What is it?" asked Max, overcome by her generosity.

"It's Pumpel's return ticket to the South of France," said Omama with tears in her eyes. "I got it refunded."

So Anna and Max had enough money after all to go to the fair.

Chapter Eleven

Papa arrived back from Paris on a Sunday, so Anna and Max went to meet him in Zurich with Mama. It was a cool, bright day in early October and as they came back with him on the steamer they could see some new snow on the mountains.

Papa was very cheerful. He had enjoyed being in Paris. Although he had stayed in a scruffy little hotel to save money he had eaten delicious food and drunk lots of good wine. All these things were cheap in France. The editor of the *Daily Parisian* had been very nice and Papa had also spoken to the editors of several French papers. They too had said that they wanted him to write for them.

"In French?" asked Anna.

"Of course," said Papa. He had had a French governess when he was small and could speak French as well as he spoke German.

"Are we all going to live in Paris then?" asked Max.

"Mama and I must talk about it first," said Papa. But he clearly thought that they should.

"How lovely!" said Anna.

"Nothing's been decided yet," said Mama. "There may be possibilities in London too."

"But it's damp there," said Anna.

Mama got quite cross. "Nonsense," she said. "You don't know anything about it."

The trouble was that Mama did not speak much French. While Papa had learned French from his French governess Mama had learned English from an English governess. The English governess had been so nice that Mama had always wanted to see the country she came from.

"We'll talk about it," said Papa. Then he told them about the people he had met—old acquaintances from Berlin who had been distinguished writers, actors or scientists and were now trying to eke out a living in France.

"One morning I ran into that actor—you remember Blumenthal?" said Papa, and Mama knew at once whom he meant. "He's opened a cake shop. His wife bakes the cakes and he serves behind the counter. I met him delivering apple strudel to a special customer." Papa smiled. "The last time I'd seen him he was the guest of honour at a banquet at the Berlin Opera."

He had also met a French journalist and his wife who had invited him several times to their home.

"They're delightful people," said Papa, "and they have a daughter about Anna's age. If we go and live in Paris I'm sure you will like them enormously."

"Yes," said Mama, but she did not sound convinced.

For the next week or two Mama and Papa talked about Paris. Papa thought that he would be able to work there and that it would be a lovely place to live. Mama who hardly knew Paris had all sorts of practical considerations like the children's education and what sort of a home they would find, to which Papa had not given much thought. In the end they agreed that she must go back to Paris with Papa and see for herself. After all, it was a very important decision.

84

"What about us?" asked Max.

He and Anna were sitting on the bed in their parents' room where they had been summoned for a discussion. Mama had the only chair and Papa was perching like a rather elegant goblin on an up-turned suitcase. It was a bit cramped but more private than downstairs.

"I think you're old enough to look after yourselves for a few weeks," said Mama.

"You mean we'd stay here on our own?" asked Anna. It seemed an extraordinary idea.

"Why not?" said Mama. "Frau Zwirn will keep an eye on you—she'll see that your clothes are clean and that you go to bed at the right time. I think you can manage the rest yourselves."

So it was settled. Anna and Max were to send their parents a postcard every other day, to let them know that everything was all right, and Mama and Papa would do the same. Mama asked them to remember to wash their necks and put on clean socks. Papa had something more serious to say to them.

"Remember that when Mama and I are in Paris you will be the only representatives of our family in Switzerland," he said. "It's a big responsibility."

"Why?" asked Anna. "What will we have to do?"

Once, at the Berlin Zoo with Onkel Julius, she had seen a small mouse-like creature with a notice on its cage claiming that it was the only representative of its species in Germany. She hoped no one was going to come and stare at her and Max.

But this was not what Papa had meant at all.

"There are Jews scattered all over the world," he said, "and the Nazis are telling terrible lies about them. So it's very important for people like us to prove them wrong."

"How can we?" asked Max.

"By being better than other people," said Papa. "For instance, the Nazis say that Jews are dishonest. So it's not enough for us to be as honest as anyone else. We have to be more honest."

(Anna at once thought guiltily of the last time she had bought a pencil in Berlin. The man in the paper shop had not charged her quite enough and Anna had not pointed out the mistake. Suppose the Nazis had got to hear of this?)

"We have to be more hard-working than other people," said Papa, "to prove that we're not lazy, more generous to prove that we're not mean, more polite to prove that we're not rude."

Max nodded.

"It may seem like a lot to ask," said Papa, "but I think it's worth it because the Jews are wonderful people and it's rather splendid to be one. And when Mama and I come back I'm sure we'll be very proud of the way you have represented us in Switzerland."

It was funny, thought Anna. Normally she hated to be told that she must be extra good, but this time she did not really mind. She had not realised before that being a Jew was so important. Secretly she resolved really to wash her neck with soap each day while Mama was away so that at least the Nazis would not be able to say that Jews had dirty necks.

However, when Mama and Papa actually left for Paris she did not feel important at all—just rather small and forlorn. She managed not to cry while she watched their train pull out of the local station, but as she and Max walked back slowly to the inn she felt quite clearly that she was too young to be left in one country while her parents went off to a different one.

"Come on, little man," said Max suddenly, "cheer up!"— and it was so funny to be addressed as "little man" which was what people sometimes called Max that she laughed.

After this things got better. Frau Zwirn had cooked her favourite lunch and it was rather grand for her and Max to eat it in the dining-room at a table all by themselves. Then Vreneli came to collect her for afternoon school and after school she and Max played with the three Zwirn children just as usual. Bed-time, which she had thought would be the worst bit, was actually very nice because Herr Zwirn came in and told them funny stories about some of the people who came to the inn. Next day she and Max were able to write quite a cheerful postcard to Mama and Papa, and one arrived for them from Paris the following morning.

After this life went along quite briskly. The postcards were a great help. Each day they either wrote to Mama and Papa or heard from them, and this made it feel as though Mama and Papa were not so far away. On Sunday Anna and Max and the three Zwirn children went into the woods to collect sweet chestnuts. They brought back great baskets full and Frau Zwirn roasted them in the oven. Then they all ate them for supper in the Zwirns' kitchen, spread thick with butter. They were delicious.

At the end of the second week after Mama and Papa's departure Herr Graupe took Anna's class on an excursion into the mountains. They spent a night high up on a mountainside, sleeping on straw in a wooden hut, and in the morning Herr Graupe got them up before it was light. He walked them along a narrow path up the mountain and suddenly Anna found that the ground under her feet had become cold and wet. It was snow.

"Vreneli, look!" she cried, and as they looked at it the snow which had been dimly grey in the darkness suddenly became brighter and pinker. It happened quite quickly and soon a rosy brilliance swept across the entire mountainside.

Anna looked at Vreneli. Her blue sweater had turned purple, her face was scarlet and even her mouse-coloured plaits glowed orange. The other children were equally transformed. Even Herr Graupe's beard had turned pink. And behind them was a huge empty expanse of deep pink snow and slightly paler pink sky. Gradually the pink faded a little and the light became brighter, the pink world behind Vreneli and the rest divided itself into blue sky and dazzling white snow, and it was fully daylight.

"You have now seen the sunrise in the Swiss mountains—the most beautiful sight in the world," said Herr Graupe as though he personally had caused it to happen. Then he marched them all down again.

It was a long walk and Anna was tired long before they got

87

to the bottom. In the train on the way back she dozed and wished that Mama and Papa were not in Paris so that she could tell them about her adventure. But perhaps there would soon be news of their return. Mama had promised that they would only stay away three weeks at the most and it was now a little more than two.

They did not get back to the inn until evening. Max had held back the regular postcard of the day and, tired as she was, Anna managed to cram a lot on it about her excursion. Then, although it was only seven o'clock, she went to bed.

On her way upstairs she came upon Franz and Vreneli whispering together in the corridor. When they saw her they stopped.

"What were you saying?" asked Anna. She had caught her father's name and something about the Nazis.

"Nothing," said Vreneli.

"Yes, you were," said Anna. "I heard you."

"Pa said we weren't to tell you," said Vreneli unhappily.

"For fear of upsetting you," said Franz. "But it was in the paper. The Nazis are putting a price on your Pa's head."

"A price on his head?" asked Anna stupidly.

"Yes," said Franz. "A thousand German Marks. Pa says it shows how important your Pa must be. There was a picture of him and all."

How could you put a thousand Marks on a person's head? It was silly. She determined to ask Max when he came up to bed but fell asleep long before.

In the middle of the night Anna woke up. It was quite sudden, like something being switched on inside her head, and she was immediately wide awake. And as though she had been thinking of nothing else all night, she suddenly knew with terrible clarity how you put a thousand Marks on a person's head.

In her mind she saw a room. It was a funny looking room because it was in France and the ceiling, instead of being solid, was a mass of criss-crossing beams. In the gaps between them something was moving. It was dark, but now the door opened and the light came on. Papa was coming to bed. He took a few steps towards the middle of the room—"Don't!" Anna wanted to cry—and then the terrible shower of heavy coins began. It came pouring down from the ceiling on to Papa's head. He called out but the coins kept coming. He sank to his knees under their weight and the coins kept falling and falling until he was completely buried under them.

So this was what Herr Zwirn had not wanted her to know. This was what the Nazis were going to do to Papa. Or perhaps, since it was in the paper, they had already done it. She lay staring into the darkness, sick with fear. In the other bed she could hear Max breathing quietly and regularly. Should she wake him? But Max hated being disturbed in the night—he would probably only be cross and say that it was all nonsense.

And perhaps it was all nonsense, she thought with a sudden lightening of her misery. Perhaps in the morning she would be able to see it as one of those silly night fears which had frightened her when she was younger—like the times when she had thought that the house was on fire, or that her heart had stopped. In the morning there would be the usual postcard from Mama and Papa, and everything would be all right.

Yes, but this was not something she had imagined—it had been in the paper . . . Her thoughts went round and round. One moment she was making complicated plans to get up, take a train to Paris and warn Papa. The next moment she thought how silly she'd look if Frau Zwirn should happen to catch her. In the end she must have fallen asleep because suddenly it was daylight and Max was already half-dressed. She stayed in bed for a moment, feeling very tired and letting the thoughts of the previous night come creeping back. After all they seemed rather unreal now that it was morning.

"Max?" she said tentatively.

Max had an open textbook on the table beside him and was looking at it while he put on his shoes and socks.

"Sorry," said Max. "Latin exam today and I haven't revised." He went back to his book, murmuring verbs and tenses. Anyway, it didn't matter, thought Anna. She was sure everything was all right.

But at breakfast there was no postcard from Mama and Papa.

"Why do you think it hasn't come?" she asked Max.

"Postal delay," said Max indistinctly through a mouthful of bread. "'Bye!" and he rushed to catch his train.

"I daresay it'll come this afternoon," said Herr Zwirn.

But she worried about it all day at school and sat chewing her pencil instead of writing a description of the sunrise in the mountains.

"What's the matter with you?" said Herr Graupe. (She usually wrote the best compositions in the class.) "It was beautiful. You should have been inspired by the experience!" And he walked away, personally offended by her lack of response to his sunrise.

There was still no postcard when she came home from school, nor was there anything in the last post at seven o'clock. It was the first time that Mama and Papa had not written. Anna managed to get through supper thinking cool thoughts about postal delays, but once she was in bed with the light out all the terror of the previous night came flooding back with such force that she felt almost choked by it. She tried to remember that she was a Jew and must not be frightened, otherwise the Nazis would say that all Jews were cowards—but it was no use. She kept seeing the room with the strange ceiling and the terrible rain of coins coming down on Papa's head. Even though she shut her eyes and buried her face in the pillow she could still see it.

She must have been making some noise in bed for Max suddenly said, "What's the matter?"

"Nothing," said Anna, but even as she said it she could feel something like a small explosion making its way up from her stomach towards her throat, and suddenly she was sobbing, "Papa . . . Papa . . ." and Max was sitting on her bed and patting her arm.

"Oh, you idiot!" he said when she had explained her fears.

90

"Don't you know what is meant by a price on someone's head?"

"Not . . . not what I thought?" said Anna.

"No," said Max. "Not at all what you thought. Putting a price on a person's head means offering a reward to anyone who captures that person."

"There you are!" wailed Anna. "The Nazis are trying to get Papa!"

"Well, in a way," said Max. "But Herr Zwirn doesn't think it's very serious—after all there's not much they can do about it as Papa isn't in Germany."

"You think he's all right?"

"Of course he's all right. We'll have a postcard in the morning."

"But supposing they sent someone after him in France— a kidnapper or someone like that?"

"Then Papa would have the whole of the French police force to protect him." Max assumed what he imagined to be a French accent. "Go away, pleeze. Ees not allowed to keednap in France. We chop off your head with the guillotine, no?"

He was such an awful mimic that Anna had to laugh and Max looked surprised at his success.

"Better go to sleep now," he said, and she was so tired that very soon she did.

In the morning instead of a postcard they had a long letter. Mama and Papa had decided that they should all live in Paris together and Papa was coming to collect them.

"Papa," said Anna after the first excitement of seeing him safe and sound had worn off. "Papa, I was a bit upset when I heard about the price on your head."

"So was I!" said Papa. "Very upset."

"Were you?" asked Anna, surprised. Papa had always seemed so brave.

"Well, it's such a very small price," explained Papa. "A thousand Marks goes nowhere these days. I think I'm worth a lot more, don't you?"

"Yes," said Anna, feeling better.

"No self-respecting kidnapper would touch it," said Papa. He shook his head sadly. "I've a good mind to write to Hitler and complain!"

Chapter Twelve

Frau Zwirn packed the children's clothes. They said good-bye
to their friends and their teachers at school and then they were
ready to leave Switzerland for their new life in France. But it
wasn't a bit like leaving Berlin, said Anna, because they would
be able to come back and see everyone at the Gasthof Zwirn any
time they liked, and Herr Zwirn had already invited them for
next summer.

They were to live in a furnished flat in Paris which Mama
was busy now getting ready. What was it like? Max wanted to
know. Papa thought for a moment. If you stood on the balcony,
he said at last, you could see the Eiffel Tower and the Arc de
Triomphe both at the same time—these were famous Paris
landmarks. But beyond this he seemed unable to remember
much about it. It was a pity, thought the children, that Papa

was sometimes so vague about practical matters. But the fact that the flat had a balcony made it sound rather grand.

The journey to Paris took the whole day and they almost did not get there at all. They had no trouble until Basle, but there they had to change trains because Basle is the frontier between Switzerland, France and Germany. Owing to some delay on the line they arrived very late and only had a few minutes to catch their Paris connection.

"We'll have to be very quick," said Papa as the train drew into the station.

Luckily there was a porter immediately at hand. He grabbed their luggage and flung it on to his wheelbarrow.

"The Paris train! Hurry!" cried Papa and the porter set off at a gallop with them all running behind him. Anna had trouble keeping the porter in sight as he turned and twisted through the crowds of people, and Max and Papa were already helping him to heave the luggage aboard the other train when she caught up with them. She stood for a moment, getting her breath back. The train must be just about to leave, for all along it people were leaning out of the windows saying good-bye to their friends on the platform. Immediately beside her a young man seemed in danger of falling right out as he gave his girl-friend a passionate farewell embrace.

"Go on with you!" said the girl and gave him a little push back into the train. As he straightened up the bottom of the window came into view. There was a printed notice stuck on it. It read STUTTGART.

"Papa!" screamed Anna. "This is the wrong train! It's going to Germany!"

"Good God!" said Papa. "Get the luggage off quick!"

He and Max dragged the suitcases off again as fast as they could. Then they heard the whistle.

"Never mind!" shouted Papa and pulled Max back, even though there was a suitcase still left on the train.

"That's our case!" shouted Max. "Please give us our case!" and just as the carriage began to move the young man with the girl-friend kindly pushed it on to the platform for them.

It landed at Anna's feet and they stood there, with luggage littered all round them, and watched the train steam out of the station.

"I clearly told you the Paris train!" said Papa, angrily looking round for the porter. But there was no sign of him. He had disappeared.

"If we'd gone on that train," asked Anna, "would we have been able to get off before it got to Germany?"

"Possibly," said Papa. "If we'd realised it was the wrong train." He put an arm round her shoulders. "I'm certainly very glad you noticed before we ever got on it."

It took some time to find another porter and Papa was sure they had missed the Paris connection, but in fact they caught it with time to spare. Its departure time had been put back to fit in with the delay on the Swiss line. It was odd that the first porter had not known about this.

As they sat in their compartment waiting for the French train to start Max suddenly said, "Papa, do you think that porter took us to the wrong train on purpose?"

"I don't know," said Papa. "It could just have been a mistake."

"I don't think it was a mistake," said Max. "I think he was trying to earn the thousand Marks on your head."

For a moment they sat thinking about it, and about what would have happened if they had travelled to Germany. Then the whistle went and the train started with a jolt.

"Well," said Papa, "if that porter really was trying to earn a thousand Marks he certainly made a bad bargain. I never had time even to give him a tip." He smiled and settled back in his seat. "And in a few minutes, thanks to Anna, we'll be not in Germany but in France. And thanks to Max we've even got all our luggage." He lifted his hands in mock admiration. "Psssh!" said Papa. "What clever children I have!"

They arrived in Paris after dark and very tired. Anna had already sensed something different in the train after leaving Basle. There had been more French voices talking quickly, sharply and incomprehensibly. The smells from the dining-car had been different too. But now that she was standing on the platform in Paris she was overwhelmed.

All round her there were people shouting, greeting each other, talking, laughing. Their lips moved quickly, their mobile faces keeping pace with them. They shrugged, embraced each other and waved their hands to emphasise what they were saying—and she could not understand a word. For a moment, in the dim light and the noise and the steam drifting back from the engine, she felt quite lost. But then Papa was bundling her and Max into a taxi and they were charging through the crowded streets.

There were lights everywhere, people walking along wide pavements, eating and drinking in the glass-fronted cafés, reading newspapers, looking into shop windows. She had forgotten a big city was like this. The height of the buildings amazed her, and the noise. As the taxi swayed and turned in the traffic, unfamiliar cars and buses and coloured electric signs which she could not read loomed out of the darkness and disappeared again.

"There's the Eiffel Tower!" cried Max—but she turned too late and missed it.

Then they were driving round a huge open space with a floodlit arch in the middle. There were cars everywhere, most of them blowing their horns.

"That's the Arc de Triomphe," said Papa. "We're nearly there."

They turned into a quieter avenue and then off it into a little narrow street, and then the taxi stopped quite suddenly with a squeal of brakes. They had arrived.

Anna and Max stood in the cold outside a tall house while Papa paid the taxi driver. Then he opened the front door and pushed them into the hall where a lady was sitting half-asleep in what appeared to be a glass-fronted cage. As soon as she saw Papa the lady leapt into life. She rushed out of what turned out to be a door in her cage and shook him by the hand, talking very quickly in French all the time. Then, still talking,

she shook hands with Max and Anna who, unable to understand, could only smile weakly in reply.

"This is Madame la concierge," said Papa. "She looks after
the house."

The taxi driver came in with the luggage and Madame la
concierge helped him to push some of it through a narrow
door which she then held open for Anna and Max. They could
hardly believe their eyes.

"Papa!" said Max. "You never told us there was a lift!"

"It's very, very grand," said Anna.

This made Papa laugh.

"I'd hardly call it that," he said. But Anna and Max were
not convinced, even when the lift creaked and groaned horribly
as it rose slowly up to the top floor. At last it stopped with a
bang and a shudder, and even before they had all got out a
door opposite them flew open and there was Mama.

Anna and Max rushed to her, and all became confusion
while she hugged them and they both tried to tell her everything that had happened since they had last seen her, and Papa
came in with the suitcases and kissed Mama, and then the
concierge brought in the rest of the cases and all at once the
tiny hall was crammed with luggage and no one could move.

"Come into the dining-room," said Mama. It was not much
bigger but the table was laid for supper and it looked bright
and inviting.

"Where can I hang my coat?" called Papa from the hall.

"There's a hook behind the door," Mama called back in
the middle of a noisy description by Max of how they had
nearly caught the wrong train. Then there was a crash as of
someone falling over something. Anna heard Papa's polite
voice saying "Good-evening", and the mild smell of burning
which Anna had noticed ever since their arrival suddenly
became intensified.

A small glum figure appeared in the doorway.

"Your fried potatoes have gone all black," it announced with
obvious satisfaction.

"Oh, Grete . . .!" cried Mama. Then she said, "This is

Grete from Austria. She is in Paris to learn French and is going to help me with the housework when she isn't studying."

Grete shook hands gloomily with Anna and Max.

"Can you speak quite a lot of French?" asked Max.

"No," said Grete. "It's a very difficult language. Some people never manage to learn it at all." Then she turned to Mama. "Well, I think I'll be off to bed."

"But Grete . . ." said Mama.

"I promised my mother that no matter what happened, I'd always get my proper sleep," said Grete. "I've turned off the gas under the potatoes. Good-night all." And she went.

"Really!" said Mama. "That girl is no use at all! Never mind, it'll be nice to have our first meal in Paris together on our own. I'll show you your room and then you can get settled in while I fry some more potatoes."

Their room was painted a rather ugly yellow and there were yellow bedspreads on the two beds. A wooden wardrobe stood in the corner. There were yellow curtains, a yellow lampshade and two chairs—nothing else. There would have been no space for any more furniture anyway because, like the dining-room, the room was quite small.

"What's outside the window?" asked Max.

Anna looked. It was not a street, as she had expected, but an inner courtyard with walls and windows all round it. It was like a well. A clanging sound far below told her there must be dustbins at the bottom, but it was too far down for her to see. Above there were only the irregular outlines of rooftops and the sky. It was very different from the Gasthof Zwirn and from their house in Berlin.

They unpacked their pyjamas and toothbrushes and decided which yellow bed would belong to whom, and then they explored the rest of the flat. Next to their room was Papa's room. It had a bed, a wardrobe, a chair and a table with Papa's typewriter on it, and it overlooked the street. From Papa's room a communicating door led to what looked like a little sitting-room, but there were some of Mama's clothes strewn about.

"Do you think this is Mama's room?" asked Anna.

"It can't be—there's no bed," said Max. There was only a sofa, a little table and two armchairs. Then Max took a closer look at the sofa.

"It's one of those special ones," he said. "Look"—and he lifted up the seat. In a cavity underneath were sheets, blankets and pillows. "Mama can sleep on it at night and then she can turn the room into a sitting-room during the day."

"It's very clever," said Anna. "It means you can use the room twice over."

Certainly it was important to make the best possible use of the space in the flat, for there was so little of it. Even the balcony which had sounded so grand when Papa talked about it was not much more than a ledge surrounded by wrought iron railings. Apart from the dining-room which they had already seen there remained only the tiny room where Grete slept, an even tinier bathroom and a small square kitchen where they found Mama and Papa.

Mama, flushed and excited, was stirring something in a bowl. Papa was leaning against the window. He looked bothered and disapproving and as the children came in they heard him say, "Surely all this trouble can't be necessary."

The kitchen was full of smoke.

"Of course it's necessary!" said Mama. "What are the children going to eat?"

"Cheese and a glass of wine," said Papa, and the children burst into laughter while Mama cried, "Oh, you are hopelessly impractical!"

"I didn't know you could cook," said Anna. She had never before seen Mama in the kitchen.

"It'll be ready in five minutes," cried Mama, stirring excitedly. "Oh, my potatoes . . . !" They were going to burn again, but she just caught them in time. "I'm making fried potatoes and scrambled eggs—I thought you'd like that."

"Lovely," said Max.

"Now where's the dish . . . and some salt . . . oh!" cried Mama, "I've got another lot of potatoes to do!" She looked

99

appealingly at Papa. "Dearest, can you pass me the colander?"

"Which is the colander?" said Papa.

By the time the meal was ready on the table it was nearly an hour later and Anna felt so tired that she no longer cared whether she ate anything or not. But she did not like to say so as Mama had gone to so much trouble. She and Max ate their supper quickly and sleepily and then fell into bed.

Through the thin walls of the flat they could hear the murmur of voices and a clattering of dishes. Mama and Papa must be clearing the table.

"You know, it's funny," said Anna just before she went to sleep. "I remember when we lived in Berlin Heimpi used to make us fried potatoes with scrambled egg. She used to say it was quick and easy."

"I expect Mama needs more practice," said Max.

Chapter Thirteen

When Anna woke up in the morning it was bright daylight. Through a gap in the yellow curtains she could see a patch of windy sky above the rooftops. There was a smell of cooking and a clicking sound which she could not at first identify, until she realised that it was Papa typing in the room next door. Max's bed was empty. He must have crept out while she was still asleep. She got up and wandered out into the hall without bothering to dress. Mama and Grete must have been busy, for all the luggage had been cleared away and through the open door she could see that Mama's bed had been turned back into a sofa. Then Mama herself appeared from the dining-room.

"There you are, my darling," she said. "Come and have some breakfast, even though it's nearly lunch-time."

Max was already installed at the dining-room table, drinking milky coffee and pulling pieces off a long and incredibly thin loaf of bread.

"It's called a *baguette*," explained Mama, "that means a stick"—which was exactly what it looked like.

Anna tried some and found it delicious. The coffee was good too. There was a red oilcloth on the table which made the cups and plates look very pretty, and the room was warm in spite of the blustery November day outside.

"It's nice here," said Anna. "We wouldn't have been able to have breakfast in our pyjamas at the Gasthof Zwirn."

"It's a bit small," said Mama. "But we'll manage."

Max stretched himself and yawned. "It's nice having our own place."

There was something more that was nice. Anna could not at first think what it was. She looked at Mama pouring coffee and at Max tilting back his chair as he had been told a hundred times not to. Through the thin walls she could hear Papa's typewriter. Then it came to her.

"I don't really mind where we are," she said—"as long as we're all together."

In the afternoon Papa took them out. They went on the Underground which was called the Metro and had a peculiar smell. Papa said it was a mixture of garlic and French cigarettes and Anna rather liked it. They saw the Eiffel Tower (but did not go up it because it would have cost too much) and the place where Napoleon was buried, and at last the Arc de Triomphe which was quite near home. By this time it was getting late, but Max noticed that you could go up to the top and that it was quite cheap, probably because it was not nearly as high as the Eiffel Tower—so they went.

No one else wanted to go to the top of the Arc de Triomphe on this cold, dark afternoon and the lift was empty. When Anna stepped out at the top she was met by an icy blast of wind and a prickle of raindrops and she wondered whether it had been a good idea to come. Then she looked down. It was as though she were standing at the centre of a huge sparkling star. Its rays stretched out in all directions and each one was a road lined with lights. When she looked closer she could see other lights which were cars and buses crawling along the roads, and immediately below they formed a bright ring circling the Arc de Triomphe itself. In the distance were the dim shapes of domes and spires and the twinkling spot which was the top of the Eiffel Tower.

"Isn't it beautiful?" said Papa. "Isn't this a beautiful city?"

Anna looked at Papa. His overcoat had lost a button and the wind was blowing through it, but Papa did not seem to notice.

"Beautiful," said Anna.

It was nice to get back to the warm flat, and this time Grete had helped Mama with the supper and it was ready in good time.

"Have you learned any French yet?" asked Mama.

"Of course not," said Grete before anyone else could answer. "It takes months."

But Anna and Max found that they had picked up quite a few words just from listening to Papa and other people. They could say *"oui"* and *"non"* and *"merci"* and *"au revoir"* and *"bonsoir Madame"*, and Max was particularly proud of *"trois billets s'il vous plaît"* which was what Papa had said when he bought tickets for the Metro.

"Well, you'll know a lot more soon," said Mama. "I've arranged for a lady to come and give you French lessons, and she's starting tomorrow afternoon."

The lady's name was Mademoiselle Martel and the following morning Anna and Max tried to collect everything they would need for her lesson. Papa lent them an old French dictionary and Mama found them some paper to write on. The only thing neither of them had was a pencil.

"You'll have to go and buy some," said Mama. "There's a shop at the corner of the street."

"But we can't speak French!" cried Anna.

"Nonsense," said Mama. "Take the dictionary with you. I'll give you a franc each and you can keep the change."

"What's the French for pencil?" asked Max.

"*Un crayon*," said Mama. Her voice did not sound as French as Papa's but she knew quite a lot of words. "Now off you go—quickly."

By the time they had travelled down in the lift by themselves—and it was Anna's turn to press the button—Anna felt quite bold about the enterprise, and her courage did not falter even when she found that the shop was rather grand and sold more office equipment than stationery. Clutching the dictionary under her arm she marched through the door ahead of Max and said in ringing tones, "*Bonsoir Madame!*"

The owner of the shop looked astonished and Max nudged her.

"That's not a *Madame*—that's a *Monsieur*," he whispered. 'And I think *bonsoir* means good evening."

"Oh!" said Anna.

But the man who owned the shop did not seem to mind. He smiled and said something in French which they could not understand. They smiled back.

Then Anna said hopefully, "*Un crayon*," and Max added, "*S'il vous plaît*."

The man smiled again, searched in a cardboard box behind the counter and produced a beautiful red pencil which he handed to Anna.

She was so amazed at her success that she forgot to say "*Merci*" and just stood there with the pencil in her hand. This was easy!

Then Max said, "*Un crayon*," because he needed one too.

"*Oui, oui*," said the man, smiling and nodding and pointing to the pencil in Anna's hand. He agreed with Max that it was a pencil.

"*Non!*" said Max. "*Un crayon!*" He sought about for a way to explain. "*Un crayon*," he cried, pointing to himself. "*Un crayon!*"

Anna giggled because it looked as though Max were introducing himself.

"Aah!" said the man. He took another pencil out of the box and handed it to Max with a little bow.

"*Merci*," said Max, much relieved. He gave the man the two francs and waited for the change. After a while it appeared that there wasn't any. Anna was very disappointed. It would have been nice to have some money.

"Let's ask him if he has any other pencils," she whispered. "They might be cheaper."

"We can't!" said Max.

"Well, let's just try," said Anna who was sometimes very pig-headed. "Look up the French for other."

Max leafed through the dictionary while the man watched him curiously. At last he found it. "It's '*autre*'," he said.

Anna smiled brightly and held out her pencil to the man. "*Un autre crayon?*" she said.

"*Oui, oui,*" said the man after a moment's hesitation. He gave her another pencil from the box. Now she had two.

"*Non,*" said Anna, handing one of the pencils back to him. His smile was getting a bit frozen. "*Un autre crayon . . .*"—she made a face and a shape with her fingers to suggest something infinitely small and unimportant.

The man stared at her to see if she was going to do anything else. Then he shrugged his shoulders and said something hopeless in French.

"Come on!" said Max, pink with embarrassment.

"No!" said Anna. "Give me the dictionary!" She turned the pages feverishly. At last she found it. Cheap . . . *bon-marché*.

"*Un bon-marché crayon!*" she cried triumphantly, startling two ladies who were examining a typewriter. "*Un bon-marché crayon, s'il vous plaît!*"

The man looked very tired. He found another cardboard box and took from it a thinner blue pencil. He gave it to Anna who nodded and gave him back the red one. Then the man gave her twenty centimes change. Then he looked questioningly at Max.

"*Oui!*" said Anna excitedly. "*Un autre bon-marché crayon!*" and the procedure was repeated with Max's pencil.

"*Merci*," said Max.

The man just nodded. He seemed worn out.

"We've got twenty centimes each," said Anna. "Think of what we'll be able to buy with that!"

"I don't think it's very much," said Max.

"Still, it's better than nothing," said Anna. She wanted to show the man that she was grateful, so as they went out of the shop she smiled at him again and said, "*Bonsoir Madame!*"

Mademoiselle Martel arrived in the afternoon—a French lady in a neat grey suit, with a shaggy pepper and salt bun. She had been a school teacher and spoke a little German, a fact which so far had been of little interest to anyone. But now Paris was suddenly crowded with refugees from Hitler, all eager to learn French, and she was run off her feet trying to give them all lessons. Perhaps, thought Anna, this was the reason for the perpetual expression of mild surprise on her slightly faded face.

She was a very good teacher. Right from the beginning she spoke French to the children nearly the whole of the time, using sign language and mime when they did not understand.

"*Le nez*", she would say, pointing to her well powdered nose, "*la main*", pointing to her hand, and "*les doigts*", wiggling her fingers. Then she would write the words down for them and they would practise spelling and pronouncing them until they knew them. Occasionally there were misunderstandings, such as when she said "*les cheveux*", pointing to her hair. Max became convinced that *cheveux* meant bun and burst into embarrassed giggles when she asked him to point out his own *cheveux*.

On the days when she did not come to give them a lesson they did home-work. At first they just learned new words but after quite a short time Mademoiselle Martel demanded that they write little stories in French.

How could they? asked Anna. They didn't know enough French.

106

Mademoiselle Martel tapped the dictionary with her finger. "*Le dictionnaire*," she said firmly.

It turned out to be a terrible struggle. They had to look up almost every word and it took Anna nearly all morning to write half a page. Then, when she showed it to Mademoiselle Martel at their next lesson, most of it was wrong anyway.

"Never mind, it will come," said Mademoiselle Martel in one of her rare excursions into German, and "Never mind, it will come!" Max said mockingly to Anna the following day, when she was still struggling after more than an hour to put down some boring incident between a dog and a cat.

"What about you? You haven't done yours yet, either," said Anna crossly.

"Yes I have," said Max. "A page and a bit."

"I don't believe it."

"Look for yourself!"

It was quite true. He had written more than a page and it all looked like French.

"What does it mean?" Anna asked suspiciously.

Max translated with a flourish.

"Once a boy had his birthday. Many people came. They had a big feast. They ate fish, meat, butter, bread, eggs, sugar, strawberries, lobsters, ice cream, tomatoes, flour . . ."

"They wouldn't eat flour," said Anna.

"You don't know what they ate," said Max. "Anyway I'm not sure that word is flour. I looked it all up at the time but I've forgotten."

"Is all this a list of what they ate?" asked Anna, pointing to the page crawling with commas.

"Yes," said Max.

"And what is this last bit?" There was just one sentence at the end which had no commas in it.

"That's the best part," said Max proudly. "I think it means 'then they all burst'."

Mademoiselle Martel read Max's composition without batting an eye-lid. She said she could see it had increased his vocabulary. But she was less pleased when, for his following day's home work, he produced an almost identical piece. This one began "Once there was a wedding," and the food the wedding guests ate was different, but it ended with everyone bursting as before. Mademoiselle Martel frowned and drummed her fingers on the dictionary. Then she told Max very firmly that he must write something different next time.

Next morning the children were sitting at the dining-room table with their books spread out on the red oilcloth as usual. Anna was wrestling with a piece about a man who had a horse and a cat. The man liked the cat and the cat liked the horse and the horse liked the man but it did not like the cat . . . It was sickening stuff to be turning out when there were so many interesting things she could have written about if only she had been able to write in German.

Max was not writing anything at all, but staring into space. When Grete came in and told them to clear their things away because she wanted to lay the table for lunch his sheet of paper was still blank.

"But it's only twelve o'clock!" cried Anna.

"I shan't have time to do it later," said Grete crossly as usual.

"Well, there's nowhere else we can work—this is the only table," said Max—and they prevailed on her, with difficulty, to let them keep it a little longer.

"What are you going to do?" asked Anna. "We want to go out this afternoon."

Max seemed to come to a decision. "Pass me the dictionary," he said.

As he leafed through it briskly (they were both becoming very practised at this) Anna heard him murmuring "funeral" under his breath.

When Mademoiselle Martel came to give them their next lesson she read Max's composition in silence. Max had done his best to introduce variety into his basic theme. The funeral guests in his story—no doubt carried away by grief—ate paper, pepper, penguins, pemmican and peaches in addition to less exotic foodstuffs, and after his usual punch-line about how they all burst at the end Max had added the words, "So there were many more funerals."

Mademoiselle Martel did not speak at all for a few moments. Then she gave Max a long, hard look and said, "Young man, you need a change."

When Mama came in at the end of the lesson as she often did to ask how the children were getting on, Mademoiselle Martel made a little speech. She said she had taught them now for three weeks and that they had made good progress. But the time had come when they would learn more by being with other children and hearing French spoken all round them.

Mama nodded. Clearly she had been thinking the same thing.

"It's nearly Christmas," she said. "Perhaps you would give them one or two more lessons before the holidays, and then they can start school."

Even Max worked hard during the remaining time. The prospect of going to a school where no one spoke anything but French was rather daunting.

And then Christmas was upon them. Grete went home to Austria for a holiday a few days before, and as Mama was busy cooking the flat soon became rather dusty. But it was so much pleasanter without Grete's grumpy presence that no one minded. Anna looked forward to Christmas and dreaded it all at the same time. She looked forward to it because you couldn't not look forward to Christmas, but she was also terribly afraid that it would make her think of Berlin and of what Christmas used to be like—what it had been like even the year before.

"Do you think we'll have a tree?" she asked Max. In Berlin there had always been a big tree in the hall, and one of the delights of Christmas had been to recognise the many coloured glass balls, the birds with the feathery tails and the trumpets which you could actually blow, as they reappeared each year to decorate it.

"I don't think the French go in for Christmas trees very much," said Max.

However, Mama managed to get one just the same. When

Papa called the children at tea-time on Christmas Eve for the celebrations to begin and they rushed into the dining-room, it was the first thing Anna saw. It was only a little tree—about two feet high—and instead of glass ornaments Mama had hung it with lametta and covered it with little candles. But it looked so pretty, shining green and silver above the red oilcloth of the table, that Anna suddenly knew that Christmas would be all right.

Presents were modest compared with previous years, but perhaps because everyone needed them more they enjoyed them just as much. Anna had a new paint box and Max a fountain pen. Omama had sent some money and Mama had bought Anna new shoes with her share. Anna had had to try them on in the shop, so they were not a surprise—but Mama had hidden them away immediately afterwards so that they would still be new for Christmas. They were thick brown leather with gold buckles and she felt very grand in them. She also had a pencil sharpener in a little case and a pair of hand-knitted red socks from Frau Zwirn, and when she thought she had seen all her presents she found one more—a very small parcel from Onkel Julius.

Anna opened it carefully and gave an exclamation of delight. "It's lovely!" she cried. "What is it?"

Nestling in the tissue paper was a short silver chain hung with tiny animals. There were a lion, a horse, a cat, a bird, an elephant and of course a monkey.

"It's a charm bracelet," said Mama, fastening it round her wrist. "How nice of Julius!"

"There's a letter with it," said Max, handing it over. Anna read it out.

"Dear Anna," it said, "I hope this little present will remind you of our many visits to the Berlin Zoo. It is not nearly so nice going there without you. Please give my love to your dear Aunt Alice. I hope she is well. Tell her I think of her often, and of her good advice which I should perhaps have taken. My love to you all. Yours, Onkel Julius."

"What does it mean?" asked Anna. "We haven't got an Aunt Alice."

Papa took the letter from her. "I think he means me," he said. "He calls me Aunt Alice because the Nazis often open letters and he could get into bad trouble if they knew that he was writing to me."

"What advice did you give him?" asked Max.

"I told him to leave Germany," said Papa and added under his breath, "Poor Julius."

"I'll write and thank him," cried Anna, "and I'll paint him a picture with my new paint box."

"Yes," said Papa, "and tell him Aunt Alice sends her love."

Then suddenly Mama made a sound with which by now they were all familiar.

"My chicken!" she cried and rushed off to the kitchen. But it had not burned and soon they were sitting down to a real Christmas dinner, all cooked by Mama. As well as the chicken there were roast potatoes and carrots, and apple flan with cream to follow. Mama was becoming quite a good cook. She had even made gingerbread hearts because they belonged to a proper German Christmas. There was something wrong with them and they had gone soggy instead of being hard and crisp, but they tasted quite nice just the same.

At the end of the meal Papa poured them all some wine and they drank a toast.

"To our new life in France!" he said and they all repeated, "To our new life in France."

Mama did not actually drink any of the wine because she said it all tasted like ink to her, but Anna liked it and drank a whole glassful. Her head felt muzzy when she finally got to bed and she had to close her eyes to stop the yellow lampshade and the wardrobe from whirling round and round.

It had been a nice Christmas, she thought. And soon she would go to school and find out what living in France was really like.

Chapter Fourteen

Anna did not go to school quite as soon as she had expected. Mama had arranged for Max to start at a *lycée* for boys early in January—a *lycée* was a French High School—but there were only very few *lycées* for girls in Paris and these were all full, with long waiting lists.

"We can't afford a private school," said Mama, "and I don't think it would be a good idea for you to go to an *école communale*."

"Why not?" asked Anna.

"They're for children who are going to leave school very early and I don't think the education is as good," said Mama. "For instance, you wouldn't be taught any Latin."

"I don't need to learn Latin," said Anna. "I'll have my

hands full trying to learn French. I'd just like to go to school!"

But Mama said, "There's no rush. Give me a little while to look around."

So Max went to school and Anna stayed at home. Max's school was almost on the other side of Paris. He had to take the Metro early in the morning and did not get back till after five. Mama had chosen it, although it was so far away, because the boys there played football twice a week. At most French schools there was no time for games—only work.

The flat seemed dull and empty on the first day without Max. In the morning Anna went with Mama to do the shopping. The weather was bright and cold and she had grown so much in the past year that there was a huge gap between the top of her knitted socks and the hem of her winter coat. Mama looked at Anna's goose-fleshy legs and sighed.

"I don't know what we're going to do about clothes for you," she said.

"I'm all right," said Anna. "I'm wearing the sweater you made me."

This sweater, owing to Mama's curious technique of knitting, had turned out so large and thick and dense that no cold could penetrate it, and was a most useful garment. The fact that only a few centimetres of Anna's skirt protruded below it did not seem to matter.

"Well, if you're sure you're warm enough we'll go to the market," said Mama. "Everything is cheaper there."

The market turned out to be some distance away and Anna carried Mama's string bag while they walked through a number of winding little streets, until at last they emerged into a bustling road lined with shops and stalls. The stalls sold everything from vegetables to haberdashery and Mama insisted on inspecting them all before she bought anything, so as to be sure of getting the best value for her money.

The owners of shops and stalls alike were crying their wares, holding them up for people to see, and sometimes it was quite difficult for Anna and Mama to walk past, as onions and beautifully clean-scrubbed carrots were thrust in front of them to admire. Some shops specialised in only a few foods. One sold nothing but cheese, and there must have been at least thirty different kinds, all carefully wrapped in muslin, displayed on a trestle table on the pavement.

Suddenly, just as Mama was about to buy a red cabbage, Anna heard a strange French voice addressing them. It belonged to a lady in a green coat. She carried a bag bulging with purchases and was smiling at Anna with very friendly brown eyes. Mama, still thinking about the cabbage, did not recognise her for a moment. Then she cried, "Madame Fernand!" in a pleased voice and they all shook hands.

Madame Fernand did not speak any German but she and Mama talked in French to each other. Anna noticed that although Mama's voice still did not sound very French she was talking more fluently than when they had first arrived. Then Madame Fernand asked Anna whether she could speak French, pronouncing the words so slowly and clearly that Anna could understand.

"A little," said Anna, and Madame Fernand clapped her hands and cried, "Very good!" and told her that she had a perfect French accent.

Mama was still holding the red cabbage which she had been about to buy and Madame Fernand took it from her gently and put it back on the stall. Then she led Mama round the corner to another stall which they must have missed and which had much better red cabbages for less money. Prompted by Madame Fernand Mama bought not only a red cabbage but quite a lot of other vegetables and fruit, and before she left them Madame Fernand presented Anna with a banana, "To strengthen her for the walk home," as Mama translated.

Mama and Anna were both much cheered by the encounter. Mama had met Madame Fernand and her journalist husband when she had first come to Paris with Papa and liked them both very much. Now Madame Fernand had asked her to ring up if she needed help or advice on anything. Her husband was going away for a few weeks but as soon as he got back she wanted Mama and Papa to come to dinner. Mama seemed very pleased at the prospect. "They're such nice people," she said, "and it would be lovely to have some friends in Paris."

They finished their shopping and carried it home. Anna said "*Bonjour Madame*," to the concierge, hoping that she would notice her perfect French accent, and chattered cheerfully to Mama on the way up in the lift. But as they entered the flat she remembered that Max was at school and the day suddenly felt dull again. She helped Mama unpack the shopping but after that she could think of nothing to do.

Grete was washing some clothes in the bathroom and for a moment Anna wondered whether to go and talk to her. But Grete was grumpier than ever since her holiday in Austria. She thought everything in France was awful. The language was impossible, the people were dirty, the food was too rich— nothing suited her. In addition Grete's mother had extracted several more promises from her during her stay at home. Apart from always having to get her proper sleep Grete had promised her mother to be careful of her back, which meant that she could only wash the floors very slowly and not at all in the corners, and not to strain her wrists. She had also promised always to have a good lunch, to rest when she was tired and never to catch cold.

Grete was very anxious to keep all these promises which were constantly being threatened by requests from Mama and the rest of the family, and they cropped up in her conversation almost as often as her disapproval of the French.

Anna did not feel she could face her just now and she wandered back to Mama in the kitchen and said, "What shall I do?"

"You could read some French," said Mama.

Mademoiselle Martel had left a book of stories for Anna to read, and she sat down in the dining-room and struggled with it for a while. But it was meant for children much younger than herself and it was depressing to sit working away with the dictionary by her side, only to discover that Pierre had thrown a stick at his little sister and that his mother had called him a naughty boy

Lunch came as a relief and Anna helped to put the things on the table and to clear them away afterwards. Then she did some painting, but still the time passed terribly slowly until at last, well after five o'clock, the door bell rang to announce Max's return. Anna rushed to let him in and found Mama already at the door.

"Well, how was it?" cried Mama.

"All right," said Max, but he looked white and tired.

"Isn't it nice?" asked Anna.

"How do I know?" said Max crossly. "I can't understand a word anyone says."

He was silent and morose for the rest of the evening. Only after supper he suddenly said to Mama, "I've got to have a proper French briefcase." He kicked the German satchel which he normally carried strapped to his back. "If I go round carrying this I even *look* different from everyone else."

Anna knew that briefcases were expensive and without thinking she said, "But your satchel was only new last year!"

"What's that to do with you?" shouted Max. "You don't know anything about it, sitting at home all day!"

"It isn't my fault that I don't go to school!" Anna shouted back. "Just because Mama can't find one for me to go to."

"Well, until you do go you can shut up!" cried Max, and after this they did not speak to each other any more even though Mama, to Anna's surprise, promised to let Max have the briefcase.

It was miserable, thought Anna. She had been looking forward to Max coming home all day, and now they'd had a row. She was determined that next day should be different, but it turned out much the same. Max came home so tired and irritable that before long they had another quarrel.

Then, to make it worse, the weather turned wet and Anna got a cold so that she could not go out. She began to feel cooped up in the flat day after day, and by evening both she and Max were so bad-tempered that they could hardly say a civil word to each other. Max felt it was unfair that he should have to struggle through long difficult days at school while Anna stayed at home, and Anna felt that Max was making enormous headway in this new world they were going to live in and worried in case she might never catch up.

"If only I could go to school—just anywhere!" Anna said to Mama.

"You can't go just anywhere," said Mama crossly. She had looked at several schools but none of them had been any good. She had even asked Madame Fernand. It was a very depressing time.

Papa was tired too. He had been working hard and had caught Anna's cold, and now he had started having nightmares again. Mama said that he had had them before, but at the Gasthof Zwirn the children had not been aware of them. He always dreamt the same thing—that he was trying to get out of Germany and was being stopped by the Nazis at the frontier. Then he woke up shouting.

Max was such a heavy sleeper that Papa's nightmares did not disturb him, even though Papa's room was next door, but Anna always heard him and it distressed her dreadfully. If Papa had woken up quickly with one big shout it would not have been so bad. But the nightmares always started slowly with Papa moaning and making frightening grunting sounds until at last they exploded into a great cry.

The first time it happened Anna thought Papa must be ill. She ran into his room and stood helplessly by his bed, calling for Mama. But even when Mama had explained to her about the nightmares and Papa had told her not to worry, she felt just as bad about them. It seemed terrible to lie in bed listening to Papa and knowing that in his dreams awful things were happening to him.

One night after she had gone to bed Anna wished very hard that Papa could stop having nightmares.

"Please, please," she whispered—for though she did not

exactly believe in God she always hoped that there might be someone who could arrange these things—"Oh please let me have the nightmares instead of Papa!" Then she lay quite still, waiting to fall asleep, but nothing happened.

Max cuddled his pillow close to his face, sighed twice and immediately dropped off. But what seemed like hours later Anna was still lying there, staring at the dark ceiling and wide awake. She began to feel very cross. How could she have a nightmare if she could not even go to sleep? She had tried doing sums in her head and to think of all sorts of boring things, but nothing had been any use. Perhaps it would help if she got up for a drink of water? But her bed was so comfortable that she decided against it.

However, she must have got up after all in the end, for she suddenly found herself in the hall. She was no longer thirsty, so she thought she would go down in the lift to see what the street looked like in the middle of the night. To her surprise she found the concierge asleep in a hammock slung across the front door and had to ease her aside in order to get out. Then the door slammed behind her—she hoped the concierge would not wake up—and she was in the street.

It was very quiet and there was a curious brown glow over everything that she had never seen before. Two men hurried past, carrying a Christmas tree.

"Better get inside," said one of them. "It's coming!"

"What's coming?" asked Anna, but the men disappeared round the corner and at the same time she could hear a shuffling sound from the opposite direction. The brown glow became stronger and then a huge, long creature heaved into view at the top of the street. Although it was so vast there was something familiar about it and Anna suddenly realised that it was Pumpel, grown to gigantic proportions. The shuffling sound was made by his legs and he looked at Anna with his little spiteful eyes and licked his lips.

"Oh, no!" said Anna.

She tried to run away, but the air had became leaden and she could not move. Pumpel started towards her.

There was a flurry of wheels and a policeman shot past on his bicycle, his cape flying behind him.

"Count its legs!" he shouted as he passed her. "It's your only chance!"

How could she count Pumpel's legs? He was like a centipede —his legs were everywhere, moving in great ripples on either side of his long body.

"One, two, three . . ." Anna began hurriedly, but it was hopeless—Pumpel was still coming towards her, and now she could see his nasty sharp teeth.

She would have to guess.

"Ninety-seven!" she cried, but still Pumpel kept coming and suddenly she realised that since they were in Paris, of course he would expect her to count in French. What was the French for ninety-seven? Her mind was blank, panicked.

"*Quatre-vingts* . . ." she stammered as Pumpel was nearly upon her . . . "*Quatre-vingts dix-sept!*" she shouted triumphantly and found herself sitting bolt-upright in bed.

Everything was quiet and she could hear Max breathing peacefully on the other side of the room. Her heart was thumping and her chest felt so tight that she could hardly move. But it was all right. She was safe. It had only been a dream.

Someone on the opposite side of the courtyard still had a light on and it made a pale golden rectangle on the curtains. She could see the dim outlines of her clothes piled on a chair ready for the morning. There was no sound from Papa's room. She lay basking in the beautiful familiarity of it all until she felt calm and sleepy. And then, with a surge of triumph, she remembered. She had had a nightmare! She had had a nightmare and Papa hadn't! Perhaps it had really worked! She snuggled down happily, and the next thing she knew it was morning and Max was getting dressed.

"Did you have any bad dreams last night?" she asked Papa at breakfast.

"Not a thing," said Papa. "I think I've got over them."

Anna never told anyone, but she always felt that it was

she who had cured Papa's nightmares—and curiously enough, after that day, neither she nor Papa had any more of them.

One evening a few days later Anna and Max had a worse row than usual. Max had come home to find Anna's drawing things all over the dining-room table and there was no room for his home-work.

"Get this rubbish out of the way!" he shouted, and Anna shouted back, "It's not rubbish! Just because you go to school, you're not the only person who matters in this house!"

Mama was talking on the telephone and she called to them through the door to be quiet.

"Well, I certainly matter a lot more than you," said Max in a fierce whisper. "You just sit about all day doing nothing!"

"I don't!" whispered Anna. "I draw and I lay the table . . ."

"I draw and I lay the table," Max mimicked her in a particularly hateful way. "You're nothing but a parasite!"

This was too much for Anna. She was not sure what a parasite was but she had a vague impression that it was something disgusting that grew on trees. As Mama put down the receiver, she burst into tears.

Mama sorted things out briskly as usual. Max must not call Anna names—anyway it was silly to call her a parasite—and Anna must clear away her things and make room for Max's home-work.

Then she added, "In any case, if Max called you a parasite just because he goes to school and you don't, there'll soon be an end to that."

Anna stopped in the middle of putting her crayons back in their box.

"Why?" she asked.

"That was Madame Fernand on the telephone," said Mama. "She says she has heard of a very good little *école communale* not too far from here. So with luck you'll be able to start next week."

Chapter Fifteen

On the following Monday Anna set off with Mama to the *école communale*. Anna was carrying her satchel and a cardboard case containing sandwiches for her lunch. Under her winter coat she wore a black pleated overall which Mama had bought her at the headmistress's suggestion. She was very proud of this overall and thought how lucky it was that her coat was too short to cover it, so that everyone could see it.

They went on the Metro, but although it was only a short distance they had to change twice. "Next time I think we'll try walking," said Mama. "It will be cheaper, too." The school was just off the Champs Elysées, a beautiful wide avenue with glittering shops and cafés, and it was surprising to find the old-fashioned gate marked *Ecole de Filles* tucked away at the back of all this grandeur. The building was dark and had clearly been there a long time. They crossed the empty playground and the sound of singing drifted down from one of the classrooms. School had already begun. As Anna climbed up the stone stairs at Mama's side to meet the headmistress she suddenly wondered what on earth it would all be like.

The headmistress was tall and brisk. She shook hands with Anna and explained something to Mama in French which Mama translated. She was sorry that there was no one who spoke German in the school but hoped that Anna would soon learn French. Then Mama said, "See you at four o'clock," and Anna could hear her heels clattering down the stairs while she was left standing in the headmistress's study.

The headmistress smiled at Anna. Anna smiled back. But it is difficult to smile at someone without talking and after a few moments her face began to feel stiff. The headmistress must have felt stiff too, for she suddenly switched her smile off. Her fingers were drumming on the desk and she seemed to be listening for something, but nothing happened, and Anna was just beginning to wonder whether they would be there all day when there was a knock at the door.

The headmistress called *"Entrez!"* and a small dark-haired girl of about Anna's own age appeared. The headmistress exclaimed something that Anna thought probably meant "at last!" and launched into a long, cross tirade. Then she turned to Anna and told her that the other girl's name was Colette and something else which might or might not have meant that Colette was going to look after her. Then she said something more and Colette started for the door. Anna, not knowing whether she was meant to follow or not, stayed where she was.

"Allez! Allez!" cried the headmistress, waving her hands at her as though she were shooing away a fly, and Colette took Anna's hand and led her out of the room.

As soon as the door closed behind them Colette made a face at it and said *"Ouf!"* Anna was pleased that she, too, found the headmistress a bit much. She hoped all the teachers were not going to be like her. Then she followed Colette along a passage and through various doors. She could hear the murmur of French voices from one of the classrooms. Others were silent— the children must be writing or doing sums. They came to a cloakroom and Colette showed her where to hang her coat, admired her German satchel and pointed out that Anna's black overall was exactly like her own—all in rapid French supplemented by sign language. Anna could not understand any of the words, but she guessed what Colette meant.

Then Colette led her through another door and Anna found herself in a large room crammed with desks. There must be at least forty girls, Anna thought. They were all wearing black overalls and this, combined with the gentle gloom of the classroom, gave the whole scene a mournful look.

The girls had been reciting something in unison, but when Anna came in with Colette they all stopped and stared at her. Anna stared back, but she was beginning to feel rather small and suddenly wondered, violently, whether she was really going to like this school. She held on tight to her satchel and her sandwich box and tried to look as though she did not care.

Then there was a hand on her shoulder. A faint smell of scent with just a tinge of garlic enveloped her and she found herself looking into a very friendly, wrinkled face surrounded by frizzy black hair.

"*Bonjour*, Anna," said the face slowly and clearly so that Anna could understand. "I am your teacher. I am called Madame Socrate."

"*Bonjour, Madame*," said Anna in a low voice.

"Very good!" cried Madame Socrate. She waved her hand towards the rows of desks and added slowly and clearly as before, "These girls are in your class," and something about "friends".

Anna removed her eyes from Madame Socrate and risked a quick glance sideways. The girls were no longer staring but smiling and she felt much better. Then Colette led her to a desk next to her own, Madame Socrate said something, and the girls—all except Anna—began to recite in unison again.

Anna sat and let the sound drone over her. She wondered what they were reciting. It was strange to be having a lesson at school without even knowing what it was about. As she listened she detected some numbers among the droning. Was it a multiplication table? No, there were not nearly enough numbers. She glanced at the book on Colette's desk. There was a picture of a king with a crown on the cover. Then it came to her, just as Madame Socrate clapped her hands for the recitation to stop. It was history! The numbers were dates and it had been a history lesson! For some reason this discovery made her feel very pleased.

The girls were now taking exercise books out of their desks and Anna was given a brand-new one. The next lesson was dictation. Anna recognised the word because once or twice Mademoiselle Martel had dictated a few simple words to her and Max. But this was a very different matter. There were long sentences and Anna had no idea what any of them meant. She did not know where one sentence ended and another began—not even where one word ended and another began. It seemed hopeless to embark on it—but it would look even worse if she just sat without writing at all. So she did what she could to translate the incomprehensible sounds into letters arranged in what seemed like possible groups. After she had covered most of a page in this strange manner the dictation came to an end, the books were collected, a bell rang and it was time for break.

Anna put on her coat and followed Colette into the playground—a paved rectangle surrounded by railings which was already filling up with other girls. It was a cold day and they were running and skipping about to keep warm. As soon as Anna appeared with Colette a number of them crowded round and Colette introduced them. There were Claudine, Marcelle, Micheline, Françoise, Madeleine . . . it was impossible to remember all their names, but they all smiled and held out their hands to Anna and she felt very grateful for their friendliness.

Then they played a singing game. They linked arms and sang and skipped forwards, backwards and sideways in time to the tune. It looked rather tame at first, but as the game went on they went faster and faster until at last they got into such a tangle that they collapsed in a heap, laughing and out of breath. The first time they did this Anna stood and watched, but the second time Colette took her hand and led her to the end of the row. She linked arms with Françoise—or it might have been Micheline—and did her best to follow the steps. When she went wrong everybody laughed, but in a friendly way. When she got it right they were delighted. She became hot and excited, and as a result of her mistakes the game ended in an even bigger muddle than before. Colette was laughing so much that she had to sit down and Anna was laughing too. She suddenly realised how long it was since she had really played with other children. It was lovely to be back at school. By the end of break she was even singing the words of the song, though she had no idea what any of them meant.

When they went back into the classroom Madame Socrate had covered the blackboard with sums and Anna's spirits rose. At least for this she did not need to know French. She worked away at them until the bell went and morning school was over.

Lunch was eaten in a small, warm kitchen under the supervision of a large lady called Clothilde. Nearly all the children lived near enough to go home to eat and there was only one other, much younger girl who stayed, apart from a little boy of about three who seemed to belong to Clothilde.

Anna ate her sandwiches but the other girl had meat, vegetables and a pudding, all of which Clothilde cheerfully heated up for her on the stove. It looked a much nicer lunch than her own and Clothilde thought so too. She made a face at the sandwiches as though they were poison, crying, "Not good! Not good!" and gave Anna to understand, with much pointing to the cooker, that another time she should bring a proper lunch.

"*Oui,*" said Anna and even ventured "*Demain*", which meant tomorrow, and Clothilde nodded her fat face and beamed.

Just as they were coming to the end of this exchange which had taken some time, the door opened and Madame Socrate came in.

"Ah," she said in her slow, clear voice. "You are speaking French. That is good."

125

Clothilde's little boy ran up to her. "I can speak French!" he cried.

"Yes, but you can't speak German," said Madame Socrate and tickled his little tummy so that he squeaked with delight.

Then she beckoned to Anna to follow her. They went back to the classroom and Madame Socrate sat down at a desk with Anna. She spread the morning's work out in front of them and pointed to the arithmetic.

"Very good!" she said. Anna had got nearly all of it right. Then Madame Socrate pointed to the dictation. "Very bad!" she said, but made such a funny face as she said it that Anna did not mind. Anna looked at her book. Her dictation had disappeared under a sea of red ink. Nearly every word was wrong. Madame Socrate had had to write the whole piece out again. At the bottom of the page it said in red, "142 mistakes" and Madame Socrate pointed to the number looking amazed and impressed, as though it were a record—which it probably was. Then she smiled, patted Anna on the back and asked her to copy the corrected version. Anna did so very carefully, and though she still could only understand very little of what she had written it was nice to have something in her book that was not all crossed out.

In the afternoon there was art and Anna drew a cat which was much admired. She gave it to Colette for being so kind to her and Colette told her in her usual mixture of quick French and dumb-show that she would pin it up on the wall of her bedroom.

When Mama came to fetch her at four o'clock Anna was very cheerful.

"How was school?" asked Mama, and Anna said, "Lovely!"

She did not realise until she got home how tired she was, but that evening, for the first time in weeks, she and Max did not have a row. It was exhausting going back to school again the next day, and the day after that, but the following day was Thursday when no one goes to school in France and she and Max both had a whole day off.

"What shall we do?" asked Max.

"Let's take our pocket money to *Prisunic*," said Anna. This was a store she and Mama had discovered on one of their shopping expeditions. Everything in it was very cheap—in fact nothing in the whole store cost more than ten francs. There were toys, household goods, stationery and even some clothes. Anna and Max spent a happy hour finding all the different things they could afford, from a cake of soap to half a pair of socks, and finally emerged with two spinning tops. In the afternoon they played with them in a little square near home till it got dark.

"Do you like your school?" Max suddenly asked as they were walking back.

"Yes," said Anna. "Everybody is very nice, and they don't mind if I can't understand what they say. Why? Don't you like yours?"

"Oh yes," said Max. "They're nice to me too, and I'm even beginning to understand French."

They walked in silence a little way and then Max suddenly burst out with, "But there's one thing I absolutely hate!"

"What?" asked Anna.

"Well—doesn't it bother you?" said Max. "I mean—being so different from everyone else?"

"No," said Anna. Then she looked at Max. He was wearing a pair of outgrown shorts and had turned them up to make them even shorter. There was a scarf dashingly tucked into the collar of his jacket and his hair was brushed in an unfamiliar way.

"You look exactly like a French boy," said Anna.

Max brightened for a moment. Then he said, "But I can't speak like one."

"Well of course you can't, after such a short time," said Anna. "I suppose sooner or later we'll both learn to speak French properly."

Max stumped along grimly.

Then he said, "Well, in my case it's definitely going to be sooner rather than later!"

He looked so fierce that even Anna who knew him well was surprised at the determination in his face.

Chapter Sixteen

One Thursday afternoon a few weeks after Anna had started
school she and Mama went to visit Great-Aunt Sarah. Great-
Aunt Sarah was Omama's sister but had married a Frenchman,
now deceased, and had lived in Paris for thirty years. Mama,
who had not seen her since she was a little girl, put on her best
clothes for the occasion. She looked very young and pretty in
her good coat and her blue hat with the veil, and as they
walked towards the Avenue Foch where Great-Aunt Sarah
lived, several people turned round to look at her.

Anna had put on her best clothes too. She was wearing the
sweater Mama had knitted, her new shoes and socks, and
Onkel Julius's bracelet, but her skirt and coat were horribly
short. Mama sighed, as always, at the sight of Anna in her
outdoor things.

"I'll have to ask Madame Fernand to do something with your coat," she said. "If you grow any more it won't even cover your pants."

"What could Madame Fernand do?" asked Anna.

"I don't know—stitch a bit of material round the hem or something," said Mama. "I wish I knew how to do these things, like her!"

Mama and Papa had been to dinner with the Fernands the previous week and Mama had come back bursting with admiration. In addition to being a wonderful cook Madame Fernand made all her own and her daughter's clothes. She had re-upholstered a sofa and made her husband a beautiful dressing-gown. She had even made him some pyjamas when he could not find the colour he wanted in the shops.

"And she does it all so easily," said Mama for whom sewing on a button was a major undertaking—"as though it weren't work at all."

Madame Fernand had offered to help with Anna's clothes, too, but Mama had felt perhaps that would be too much to accept. Now, however, seeing Anna stick out of her coat in all directions, she changed her mind.

"I will ask her," she said. "If she just showed me how to do it perhaps I could manage it myself."

By this time they had arrived at their destination. Great-Aunt Sarah lived in a large house set back from the road. They had to cross a courtyard planted with trees to reach it and the concierge who directed them to her flat wore a uniform with gold buttons and braid. Great-Aunt Sarah's lift was made of plate glass and carried them swiftly upwards without any of the groans and shudders Anna was used to, and her front door was opened by a maid in a frilly white apron and cap.

"I'll tell Madam you're here," said the maid, and Mama sat on a little velvet chair while the maid went into what must be the drawing-room. As she opened the door they could hear a buzz of voices and Mama looked worried and said, "I hope this is the right day . . ." But almost at once the door opened again and Great-Aunt Sarah ran out. She was a stout old lady but she moved at a brisk trot and for a moment Anna wondered whether she would be able to stop when she reached them.

"Nu," she cried, throwing her heavy arms round Mama. "So here you are at last! Such a long time I haven't seen you—and such dreadful things happening in Germany. Still, you're safe and well and that's all that matters." She relapsed into another velvet chair, overflowing on all sides, and said to Anna, "Do you know that the last time I saw your Mama she was only a little girl? And now she has a little girl of her own. What's your name?"

"Anna," said Anna.

"Hannah—how nice. A good Jewish name," said Great-Aunt Sarah.

"No, Anna," said Anna.

"Oh, Anna. That's a nice name too. You must excuse me," said Great-Aunt Sarah, leaning perilously towards her on the little chair, "but I'm a bit deaf." Her eyes took in Anna properly for the first time and she looked astonished. "Goodness, child," she exclaimed. "Such long legs you have! Aren't they cold?"

"No," said Anna. "But Mama says if I grow any more my coat won't even cover my pants."

As soon as the words were out of her mouth, she wished she had not said them. It was not the sort of thing one said to a great-aunt one hardly knew.

"What?" said Great-Aunt Sarah.

Anna could feel herself blushing.

"A moment," said Great-Aunt Sarah and suddenly, from somewhere about her person, she produced an object like a trumpet. "There," she said, putting the thin end not to her mouth as Anna had half-expected, but to her ear. "Now say it again, child—very loudly—into my trumpet."

Anna tried desperately to think of something quite different that she could say instead and that would still make sense, but her mind remained blank. There was nothing for it.

"Mama says," she shouted into the ear trumpet, "that if I grow any more my coat won't even cover my pants!"

When she withdrew her face she could feel that she had gone scarlet.

Great-Aunt Sarah seemed taken aback for a moment. Then her face crumpled up and a noise somewhere between a wheeze and a chuckle escaped from it.

"Quite right!" she cried, her black eyes dancing. "Your Mama is quite right! But what is she going to do about it, eh?" Then she added to Mama, "Such a funny child—such a nice funny child you have!" And rising from the chair with surprising agility she said, "So now you must come and have some tea. There are some old ladies here who have been playing Bridge, but I'll soon get rid of them"—and she led the way, at a gentle gallop, into the drawing-room.

The first thing that struck Anna about Great-Aunt Sarah's old ladies was that they all looked a good deal younger than Great-Aunt Sarah. There were about a dozen of them, all elegantly dressed with elaborate hats. They had finished playing Bridge—Anna could see the card tables pushed back against the wall—and were now drinking tea and helping themselves to tiny biscuits which the maid was handing round on a silver tray.

"Every Thursday they come," whispered Great-Aunt Sarah in German. "Poor old things, they have nothing better to do. But they're all very rich and they give me money for my needy children."

Anna, who had only just got over her surprise at Great-Aunt Sarah's old ladies, found it even more difficult to imagine her with needy children—or indeed with any children at all—but she did not have time to ponder the problem for she was being loudly introduced along with Mama.

"My niece and her daughter have come from Germany," shouted Great-Aunt Sarah in French but with a strong German accent. "Say bongshour!" she whispered to Anna.

"*Bonjour*," said Anna.

Great-Aunt Sarah threw up her hands in admiration. "Listen to the child!" she cried. "Only a few weeks she has been in Paris and already she speaks French better than I!"

Anna found it difficult to keep up this impression when one of the ladies tried to engage her in conversation, but she was saved from further efforts when Great-Aunt Sarah's voice boomed out again.

"I have not seen my niece for years," she shouted, "and I have been longing to have a talk with her."

At this the ladies hurriedly drank up their tea and began to make their farewells. As they shook hands with Great-Aunt Sarah they dropped some money into a box which she held out to them, and she thanked them. Anna wondered just how many needy children Great-Aunt Sarah had got. Then the maid escorted the ladies to the door and at last they had all disappeared.

It was nice and quiet without them, but Anna noticed with regret that the silver tray with the little biscuits had disappeared along with the ladies and that the maid was gathering up the empty cups and carrying them out of the room. Great-Aunt Sarah must have forgotten her promise of tea. She was sitting on the sofa with Mama and telling her about her needy children. It turned out that they were not her own after all but a charity for which she was collecting money, and Anna who had briefly pictured Great-Aunt Sarah with a secret string of ragged urchins felt somehow cheated. She wriggled restlessly in her chair, and Great-Aunt Sarah must have noticed for she suddenly interrupted herself.

"The child is bored and hungry," she cried and added to the maid, "Have the old ladies all gone?"

The maid replied that they had.

"Well then," cried Great-Aunt Sarah, "you can bring in the real tea!"

A moment later the maid staggered back under a tray loaded with cakes. There must have been five or six different kinds, apart from an assortment of sandwiches and biscuits. There was also a fresh pot of tea, chocolate and whipped cream.

"I like cakes," said Great-Aunt Sarah in answer to Mama's look of astonishment, "but it's no use offering them to those old ladies—they're much too careful of their diets. So I thought we'd have our tea after they'd gone." So saying she slapped a large portion of apple flan on to a plate, topped it with whipped cream and handed it to Anna. "The child needs feeding," she said.

During tea she asked Mama questions about Papa's work and about their flat, and sometimes Mama had to repeat her answers into the ear-trumpet. Mama talked about everything quite cheerfully, but Great-Aunt Sarah kept shaking her head and saying, "To have to live like this . . . such a distinguished man . . . !" She knew all Papa's books and bought the *Daily Parisian* specially to read his articles. Every so often she would look at Anna, saying, "And the child—so skinny!" and ply her with more cake.

At last, when no one could eat any more, Great-Aunt Sarah heaved herself out from behind the tea-table and set off at her usual trot towards the door, beckoning to Mama and Anna to follow. She led them to another room which seemed to be entirely filled with cardboard boxes.

"Look," she said. "All this I have been given for my needy children."

The boxes were filled with lengths of cloth in all sorts of different colours and thicknesses.

"One of my old ladies is married to a textile manufacturer," explained Great-Aunt Sarah. "So he is very rich and he gives me all the ends of material he does not want. Now I have an idea—why shouldn't the child have some of it? After all it is for needy children, and she is as needy as most."

"No, no," said Mama, "I don't think I could . . ."

"Ach—always so proud," said Great-Aunt Sarah. "The child needs new clothes. Why shouldn't she have some?"

She rummaged in one of the boxes and pulled out some thick woollen material in a lovely shade of green. "Just nice for a coat," she said, "and a dress she needs, and perhaps a skirt . . ."

In no time at all she had assembled a pile of cloth on the bed, and when Mama tried again to refuse she only cried, "Such nonsense! You want the police should arrest the child for going about with her pants showing?"

At this Mama, who had in any case not been protesting very hard, had to laugh and give in. The maid was asked to wrap it all up, and when it was time to leave Mama and Anna each had a big parcel to carry.

"Thank you very, very much!" Anna shouted into Great-Aunt Sarah's ear-trumpet. "I've always wanted a green coat!"

"I wish you luck to wear it!" Great-Aunt Sarah shouted back.

Then they were outside, and as Anna and Mama walked back in the dark they talked all the way about the different pieces of material and what they could be made into. As soon as they got home Mama telephoned Madame Fernand who was delighted and said they must bring everything round the following Thursday for a great dress-making session.

"Won't it be lovely!" cried Anna. "I can't wait to tell Papa!"—and just then Papa came in. She told him excitedly what had happened. "And I'll be able to have a dress and a coat," she gabbled, "and Great-Aunt Sarah just gave it to us because it was meant for needy children and she said I was as needy as most, and we had a lovely tea and . . ."

She stopped because of the expression on Papa's face.

"What is all this?" he said to Mama.

"It's just as Anna told you," said Mama, and there was something careful about her voice. "Great-Aunt Sarah had a whole lot of cloth which had been given to her and she wanted Anna to have some."

"But it had been given to her for needy children," said Papa.

"That's only what it was called," said Mama. "She's interested in various charities—she's a very kind woman . . ."

"Charities?" said Papa. "But we can't accept charity for our children."

"Oh, why must you always be so difficult?" shouted Mama. "The woman is my aunt and she wanted Anna to have some clothes—that's all there is to it!"

"Honestly, Papa, I don't think she meant it in any way you wouldn't like," Anna put in. She was feeling miserable and almost wished she had never seen the cloth.

"It's a present for Anna from a relative," said Mama.

"No," said Papa. "It's a present from a relative who runs a charity—a charity for needy children."

"All right then, we'll give it back!" shouted Mama. "If that's what you want! But will you tell me what the child is going to wear? Do you know the price of children's clothes in the shops? Look at her—just look at her!"

Papa looked at Anna and Anna looked back at him. She wanted the new clothes but she did not want Papa to feel so badly about them. She tugged at her skirt to make it look longer.

"Papa . . ." she said.

"You do look a bit needy," said Papa. His face looked very tired.

"It doesn't matter," said Anna.

"Yes, it does," said Papa. "It does matter." He fingered the stuff in the parcels. "Is this the cloth?"

She nodded.

"Well then, you'd better get it made up into some new clothes," said Papa. "Something warm," he said and went out of the room.

In bed that night Anna and Max lay talking in the dark.

"I didn't know we were needy," said Anna. "Why are we?"

"Papa doesn't earn a lot," said Max. "The *Daily Parisian* can't afford to pay him very much for his articles and the French have their own writers."

"They used to pay him a lot in Germany."

"Oh yes."

For a while they lay without talking. Then Anna said, "Funny, isn't it?"

"What?"

"How we used to think we'd be back in Berlin within six months. We've been away more than a year already."

"I know," said Max.

Suddenly, for no particular reason, Anna remembered their old house so vividly that she could almost see it. She remembered what it felt like to run up the stairs and the little patch on the carpet on the landing where she had once spilt some ink, and how you could see the pear tree in the garden from the windows. The nursery curtains were blue and there was a white-painted table to write or draw on and Bertha the maid had cleaned it all every day and there had been a lot of toys . . . But it was no use going on thinking about it, so she closed her eyes and went to sleep.

Chapter Seventeen

The dress-making session at the Fernands was a great success. Madame Fernand was just as nice as Anna remembered her, and she cut out Great-Aunt Sarah's cloth so cleverly that there was enough for a pair of grey shorts for Max as well as a coat, a dress and a skirt for Anna. When Mama offered to help with the sewing Madame Fernand looked at her and laughed.

"You go and play the piano," she said. "I'll get on with this."

"But I've even brought some sewing things," said Mama. She dug in her handbag and produced an elderly reel of white cotton and a needle.

"My dear," said Madame Fernand quite kindly, "I wouldn't trust you to hem a handkerchief."

So Mama played the piano at one end of the Fernands' pleasant sitting-room while Madame Fernand sewed at the other, and Anna and Max went off to play with the Fernands' daughter Francine.

Max had had grave doubts about Francine before they came.

"I don't want to play with a girl!" he had said, and even claimed that he could not come because of his home-work.

"You've never been so keen on your home-work before!" said Mama crossly, but it was not really fair because lately, in his efforts to learn French as fast as possible, Max had become much more conscientious about school. He was deeply offended and scowled at everyone until they arrived at the Fernands' flat and Francine opened the door for them. Then his scowl quickly disappeared. She was a remarkably pretty girl with long honey-coloured hair and large grey eyes.

"You must be Francine," said Max and added untruthfully but in surprisingly good French, "I have so much looked forward to meeting you!"

Francine had quite a lot of toys and a big white cat. The cat immediately took possession of Anna and sat on her lap while Francine searched for something in her toy cupboard. At last she found it.

"This is what I got for my birthday," she said and produced a games compendium very like the one Anna and Max had owned in Germany.

Max's eyes met Anna's over the cat's white fur.

"Can I see?" he asked and had it open almost before Francine agreed. He took a long time looking at the contents, fingering the dice, the chessmen, the different kinds of playing cards.

"We used to have a box of games like this," he said at last. "Only ours had dominoes as well."

Francine looked a little put out at having her birthday present belittled.

"What happened to yours?" she asked.

"We had to leave it behind," said Max and added gloomily, "I expect Hitler plays with it now."

Francine laughed. "Well, you'll have to use this one instead," she said. "As I have no brothers or sisters I don't often have anyone to play with."

138

After this they played Ludo and Snakes and Ladders all afternoon. It was nice because the white cat sat on Anna's lap and there was no need for her to speak much French during the games. The white cat seemed quite happy to have dice thrown over its head and did not want to get down even when Madame Fernand called Anna to try on the new clothes. For tea it ate a bit of iced bun which Anna gave it, and afterwards it climbed straight back on to her lap and smiled at her through its long white fur. When it was time to leave it followed her to the front door.

"What a pretty cat," said Mama when she saw it.

Anna was longing to tell her how it had sat on her lap while she had played Ludo but thought it would be rude to speak German when Madame Fernand could not understand it. So, very haltingly, she explained in French.

"I thought you told me Anna spoke hardly any French," said Madame Fernand.

Mama looked very pleased. "She is beginning to," she said.

"Beginning to!" exclaimed Madame Fernand. "I've never seen two children learn a language so fast. Max sounds almost like a French boy at times and as for Anna—only a month or two ago she could hardly say a word, and now she understands everything!"

It was not quite true. There were still a lot of things Anna could not understand—but she was delighted just the same. She had been so impressed with Max's rapid progress that she had not noticed how much she herself had improved.

Madame Fernand wanted them all to come again the following Sunday so that Anna could have a final fitting, but Mama said, no, next time all the Fernands must come to them—and thus began a series of visits which both families found so pleasant that it soon became a regular arrangement.

Papa especially enjoyed Monsieur Fernand's company. He was a large clever-looking man and often, while the children played in the dining-room at home, Anna could hear his deep voice and Papa's in the bedroom-turned-sitting-room next door. They seemed to have endless things to talk about and sometimes

Anna could hear them laughing loudly together. This always pleased her because she had hated the tired look on Papa's face when he had heard about Great-Aunt Sarah's cloth. She had noticed since that this look occasionally returned— usually when Mama was talking about money. Monsieur Fernand was always able to keep the look at bay.

The new clothes were soon finished and turned out to be the nicest Anna had ever had. She went to show them to Great-Aunt Sarah the very first time she wore them and took with her a poem she had composed specially as a thanks offering. It described all the clothes in detail and ended with the lines,

"And so I am the happy wearer

Of all these nice clothes from Aunt Sarah."

"Goodness, child," said Great-Aunt Sarah when she read it. "You'll be such a writer yet, like your father!"

She seemed terribly pleased with it.

Anna was pleased too because somehow the poem seemed to make it quite definite that the gift of cloth had not been charity—and also it was the first time she had ever managed to write a poem about anything other than a disaster.

Chapter Eighteen

In April it suddenly became spring, and though Anna tried
to go on wearing the beautiful green coat which Madame
Fernand had made for her she soon found it much too thick.

Walking to school became a delight on these bright, sunny
mornings, and as the Parisians opened their windows to let
in the warm air all sorts of interesting smells escaped and
mingled with the scent of spring in the streets. Apart from the
usual hot garlicky breath rising from the Metro she suddenly
encountered delicious waftings of coffee, freshly baked bread,
or onions being fried ready for lunch. As the spring advanced
doors were opened as well as windows, and while walking down
the sunlit streets she could glimpse the dim interiors of cafés
and shops which had been invisible all through the winter.
Everyone wanted to linger in the sunshine, and the pavements
in the Champs Elysées became a sea of tables and chairs

amongst which white-coated waiters flew about, serving drinks to their customers.

The first of May was called the day of the lily-of-the-valley. Baskets piled high with the little green and white bunches appeared at every street corner and the cries of the vendors echoed everywhere. Papa had an early appointment that morning and walked part of the way to school with Anna. He stopped to buy a paper from an old man at a kiosk. There was a picture of Hitler on the front page, making a speech, but the old man folded the paper in half so that Hitler disappeared. Then he sniffed the air appreciatively and smiled, showing one tooth.

"It smells of spring!" he said.

Papa smiled back and Anna knew that he was thinking how lovely it was to be spending this spring in Paris. At the next corner they bought some lily-of-the-valley for Mama without even asking first how much they cost.

The school building seemed dark and chilly after the brightness outside, but Anna looked forward each morning to seeing Colette, who had become her special friend, and her teacher Madame Socrate. Though she still found the school day long and tiring she was beginning to understand more of what was going on. The mistakes in her dictations had gradually been reduced to fifties instead of hundreds. Madame Socrate continued to help her during the lunch break, and she now managed sometimes to answer a question in class.

At home Mama was becoming a really good cook, helped with advice from Madame Fernand, and Papa said he had never eaten so well in his life. The children learned to enjoy all sorts of food they had never even heard of before and to drink a mixture of wine and water with their meals, like French children. Even fat Clothilde in the school kitchen approved of the lunches Anna brought for her to reheat.

"Your mother knows how to do things," she said, and Mama was delighted when Anna told her.

Only Grete remained gloomy and discontented. No matter what Mama served up she always compared it unfavourably with some Austrian version of the same dish, and if it was something you could not get in Austria Grete did not think you should eat it at all. She had an amazing resistance to everything French and did not seem to get any better at speaking the language even though she went to classes every day. Since the promises she had made to her mother continued to prevent her from being of much help to Mama, everyone, including Grete, looked forward to the time when she would return to Austria for good.

"And the sooner the better," said Madame Fernand who had been able to observe Grete at close quarters, for the two families still spent most of their Sundays together. As spring turned into summer, instead of meeting at their homes they went out to the Bois de Boulogne which was a large park not too far away and the children played ball games on the grass. Once or twice Monsieur Fernand borrowed a friend's car and drove them all out to the country for a picnic. To Anna's joy the cat came too on these occasions. It did not seem to mind being put on a lead and while Francine chattered to Max, Anna proudly took charge of it, holding on to the lead when the cat wanted to climb a tree or a lamp-post and following with the lead held high above her head when the cat decided to walk along the top of some railings instead of along the bottom.

In July it became very hot—much hotter than it had ever been in Berlin. There seemed no air at all in the little flat even though Mama kept all the windows open all the time. The children's bedroom especially was stifling and the courtyard it overlooked seemed almost hotter than the inside. It was difficult to sleep at night and nobody could concentrate on lessons at school. Even Madame Socrate was tired. Her frizzy black hair went limp with the heat and everyone longed for the end of term.

On the fourteenth of July not only the schools but the whole of France had a holiday. It was the anniversary of the French Revolution, and there were flags everywhere and fireworks in the evening. Anna and Max went to see them with their parents and the Fernands. They took the Metro which was packed with cheerful people, and among a crowd of other Parisians they climbed a long flight of steps up to a church on top of a hill. From here they could see right across Paris, and as the fireworks began to explode against the dark blue sky everyone shouted and cheered. At the end of the display someone started to sing the *Marseillaise*, then someone else joined in, and soon the whole huge crowd was singing together in the hot night air.

"Come on, children!" cried Monsieur Fernand, and Anna and Max joined in too. Anna thought it sounded wonderful, especially an unexpected slow bit that came in the middle of the song, and she was sorry when it ended.

The crowds began to leak away down the steps and Mama said, "Home to bed!"

"Good heavens, you can't send them to bed now. It's the fourteenth of July!" cried Monsieur Fernand. Mama protested that it was late, but the Fernands only laughed at her.

"It's the fourteenth of July," they said, as though this explained everything. "The evening has hardly begun!"

Mama looked doubtfully at the children's excited faces. "But what . . . ?" she began.

"First," said Monsieur Fernand, "we are going to eat."

Anna was under the impression that they had eaten already, for they had had boiled eggs before they came out—but clearly this was not the sort of eating Monsieur Fernand had in mind. He took them to a large busy restaurant where they sat at a table outside on the pavement and ordered a meal.

"Snails for the children!" cried Monsieur Fernand. "They've never tried them."

Max stared at his portion in horror and could not bring himself to touch them. But Anna, encouraged by Francine, tried one and found that it tasted like a very delicious mushroom. In the end she and Francine ate Max's snails as well as their own. Towards the end of the meal, while they were spooning up cream puffs, an old man arrived with a stool and an accordion. He sat down and began to play, and soon some of the people left their tables to dance in the street. A cheerful looking sailor appeared at Mama's side and invited her to dance. Mama was surprised at first but then she accepted and Anna watched her being whirled round and round, still looking astonished but pleased. Then Monsieur Fernand danced with Francine, and Anna danced with Papa, and Madame Fernand said she did not feel like dancing just yet because she could see that Max would absolutely hate it, and after a while Monsieur Fernand said, "Let's move on."

It was cooler now and Anna did not feel at all tired as they wandered through the crowded streets. There were accordions and people dancing everywhere, and every so often they stopped and joined in. Some cafés were serving free wine to celebrate the occasion and when they felt like a rest the grown-ups stopped for a drink and the children had cassis, which was blackcurrant juice. They saw the river shining in the moonlight and the cathedral of Notre Dame squatting like a great dark creature in the middle. At one time they walked along the bank and under the bridges, and there were accordion players and people dancing here too. They went on and on until Anna lost all sense of time and just followed Monsieur Fernand in a happy daze.

Suddenly Max said, "What is that funny light in the sky?"

It was the dawn.

By this time they had reached the main Paris market, and carts loaded with fruit and vegetables were rumbling over the cobblestones all about them.

"Hungry?" asked Monsieur Fernand.

It was ridiculous since they had already eaten two suppers, but everyone was starving. There was no accordion music here, only people getting ready for the day's work, and a woman in a small café was serving bowls of steaming onion soup. They ate great bowlfuls, sitting on wooden benches with the market people, and mopped up the remains with hunks of bread. When they came out of the café it was daylight.

"Now you can put the children to bed," said Monsieur Fernand. "They have seen the fourteenth of July."

After a sleepy farewell they rode home on the Metro among late revellers like themselves and people going to work, and collapsed into their beds.

"We never had a fourteenth of July in Germany," said Anna just before she fell asleep.

"Well, of course not," said Max. "We didn't have the French Revolution!"

"I know that," said Anna crossly and added, just as sleep was about to overtake her, "But wasn't it lovely!"

Then the summer holidays were upon them. Just as they were wondering how to spend them, a letter arrived from Herr Zwirn inviting the whole family to the Gasthof Zwirn as his guests—and just as they were wondering where to get the money for the fares, Papa was asked to write three articles for a French newspaper. This paper paid him so much more than his normal fees from the *Daily Parisian* that it solved the problem.

Everyone was delighted at the prospect, and to top it all on the last day of term Max brought home a good report. Mama and Papa could hardly believe their eyes when they saw it. There was not a single "Does not try" or "Shows no interest". Instead there were words like "intelligent" and "hard-working" and the headmaster's comment at the bottom of the sheet said that Max had made remarkable progress. This made Mama feel so cheerful that she absent-mindedly bade quite a fond farewell to Grete, who was going back to Austria at last. They were all so pleased to get rid of her that they felt they must be extra nice to her, and Mama even gave her a small scarf.

"I don't know if this sort of thing is worn in Austria," said Grete glumly when she saw it, but she took it anyway. And then they themselves set off for Switzerland.

The Gasthof Zwirn was quite unchanged. Herr and Frau Zwirn were as kind and warm-hearted as ever, and after the heat in Paris the air by the lake was wonderfully fresh. It was

146

nice to hear the familiar German-Swiss dialect and to be able to understand everything people said instead of only half, and Franz and Vreneli were ready to pick up their friendships with Anna and Max exactly where they had left off. In no time at all Vreneli was bringing Anna up to date about the red-haired boy who had apparently taken to looking at Vreneli in a certain way—a warm sort of way, said Vreneli—which she could not describe but which appeared to please her. Franz carried Max off to fish with the same old fishing rod, and they all played the same games and walked along the same paths in the woods which they had enjoyed so much the previous year. It was all exactly as it had been, and yet there was something about this very sameness that made Anna and Max feel a little like strangers. How could the Zwirns' lives have stayed so much the same when their own had become so different?

"You'd think just something would have changed," said Max, and Franz asked, "What sort of thing?" But Max did not know himself.

One day Anna was walking through the village with Vreneli and Roesli when they met Herr Graupe.

"Welcome back to our beautiful Switzerland!" he cried, shaking her hand enthusiastically, and soon he was asking her all sorts of questions about school in France. He was convinced that nothing could compare with his own village school and Anna found herself sounding almost apologetic when she explained that she liked it all very much.

"Really?" said Herr Graupe incredulously, while she described the work, and her lunches with Clothilde in the school kitchen, and Madame Socrate.

And then an odd thing happened to her. Herr Graupe was asking her something about the French school-leaving age which she did not know—but instead of telling him so in German she found herself suddenly shrugging her shoulders and saying "*Je ne sais pas*" in her best Parisian accent. She was horrified as soon as she had said it. She knew he would think that she was showing off. But she hadn't been. She could not even understand where the words had come from. It was as though somewhere inside her something were secretly thinking in French—and that was ridiculous. Since she had never been able to think in French in Paris, why should she suddenly start now?

"I see we're becoming quite French already," said Herr Graupe disapprovingly when they had both recovered from their surprise at her reply. "Well—I mustn't keep you." And he hurried off.

Vreneli and Roesli were both unusually quiet when the three of them walked back together.

"I suppose you can speak French like anything now," said Vreneli at last.

"No," said Anna. "Max is much better."

"I can say *Oui*—I think that means Yes, doesn't it?" said Roesli. "Are there any mountains in France?"

"Not near Paris," said Anna.

Vreneli had been staring at Anna thoughtfully. Then she said, "You know, you're different somehow."

"I'm not!" said Anna indignantly.

"But you are," said Vreneli. "I don't know what it is but you've changed."

"Nonsense!" cried Anna. "Of course I haven't!" But she knew that Vreneli was right and suddenly, though she was only eleven, she felt quite old and sad.

The rest of the holidays passed happily enough. The children bathed and played with the Zwirns, and if it was not quite as it had been it was still very pleasant. After all, what did it matter, said Max, that they no longer quite belonged? They were sorry to leave at the end of the summer and took a long and affectionate farewell from their friends. But to both Anna and Max, going back to Paris felt more like going home than they would ever have thought possible.

Chapter Nineteen

When Anna went back to school she found that she had been moved up. Madame Socrate was still her teacher but the work was suddenly much harder. This was because her class was preparing for an examination called the *certificat d'études* which everyone except Anna was taking the following summer.

"I'm excused because I'm not French," Anna told Mama, "and anyway I couldn't possibly pass."

But she had to do the work just the same.

The girls in her class were expected to do at least an hour's home-work each day after school, to learn whole pages of history and geography by heart, to write essays and study grammar—and Anna had to do it all in a language which she still did not completely understand. Even arithmetic which had been her great stand-by now let her down. Instead of sums which needed no translation her class were doing problems—long complicated tangles in which people dug ditches and passed each other in trains and filled tanks with water at one rate while siphoning it off at another—and all this she had to translate into German before she could even begin to think about it.

As the weather became colder and the days darker she began to feel very tired. She dragged her feet walking home from school and then just sat and stared at her home-work instead of getting on with it. She suddenly felt quite discouraged. Madame Socrate, mindful of the coming exam, no longer had so much time for her, and her work seemed to be getting worse rather than better. No matter what she did, she could not reduce the mistakes in her dictations below forty—lately they had even climbed up again into the fifties. In class, even though she often knew the answers, it took her so long to translate them into French in her mind that it was usually too late to give them. She felt that she would never be able to catch up and was getting tired of trying.

One day when she was sitting over her home-work Mama came into the room.

"Have you nearly finished?" she asked.

"Not quite," said Anna, and Mama came and looked at her book.

It was arithmetic home-work and all Anna had written was the date and "Problems" at the top of the page. She had drawn a little box-shape round "Problems" with a ruler and had followed this with a wavy line in red ink. Then she had decorated the wavy line with dots and surrounded it with a zigzag shape and more dots in blue. All this had taken her the best part of an hour.

At the sight of it Mama exploded.

"No wonder you can't do your home-work!" she shouted. "You put it off and put it off until you're too tired to make any sense of it! You'll never learn anything at this rate!"

This was so exactly what Anna felt herself that she burst into tears.

"I do try!" she sobbed. "But I just don't seem to be able to do it. It's too difficult! I try and try and it isn't any use!"

And in another burst of weeping she dripped tears all over "Problems" so that the paper cockled and the wavy line spread and got mixed up with the zig-zag.

"Of course you can do it!" said Mama, reaching for the book. "Look, if I help you . . ."

But Anna shouted "No!" quite violently and pushed the book away so that it shot off the table and on to the floor.

"Well, you're obviously in no condition to do any home-work today," said Mama after a moment's silence and walked out of the room.

Anna was just wondering what she ought to do when Mama came back again with her coat on.

"I have to buy some cod for supper," she said. "You'd better come with me and get some fresh air."

They walked down the street together without talking. It was cold and dark and Anna trudged along beside Mama with her hands in her pockets, feeling quite empty. She was no good. She would never be able to speak French properly. She would be like Grete who had never managed to learn, but unlike Grete she could not go home to her own country. At this thought she began to blink and sniff all over again, and Mama had to grab her arm to stop her bumping into an old lady.

The fish shop was some distance away in a brightly lit, busy street. There was a cake shop next to it, its window filled with creamy delicacies which you could either take away or sit down to eat at one of the little tables inside. Anna and Max had often admired it, but neither had ever set foot inside it because it was so expensive. This time Anna was too miserable even to look at it, but Mama stopped by the heavy glass door.

"We'll go in here," she said to Anna's surprise and steered her through.

They were met by a wave of warm air and a delicious smell of pastries and chocolate.

"I'll have a cup of tea and you can have a cake," said Mama, "and then we'll have a talk."

"Isn't it too expensive?" asked Anna in a small voice.

"We can manage one cake," said Mama. "But you'd better

151

not pick one of those absolutely enormous ones, otherwise we might not have enough money left for the cod."

Anna chose a pastry filled with sweet chestnut purée and whipped cream, and they sat down at one of the little tables.

"Look," said Mama as Anna sank her fork into the cake, "I know it's difficult for you at school and I know you've tried. But what are we to do? We're living in France and you have to learn French."

"I get so tired," said Anna, "and I'm getting worse instead of better. Perhaps I'm just one of those people who can't learn languages."

Mama was up in arms at once.

"Nonsense!" she said. "There's no such thing at your age!"

Anna tried a bit of her pastry. It was delicious.

"Would you like some?" she said.

Mama shook her head.

"You've done very well so far," she said after a moment. "Everyone tells me your French accent is perfect, and you really know an awful lot considering that we've been here less than a year."

"It's just that now I don't seem to be able to get any further," said Anna.

"But you will!" said Mama.

Anna looked down at her plate.

"Look," said Mama, "these things don't always happen as you expect. When I was studying music I sometimes struggled with something for weeks without getting anywhere at all—and then suddenly, just when I felt it was quite hopeless, the whole thing became clear and I couldn't think why I hadn't seen it before. Perhaps it will be like that with your French."

Anna said nothing. She did not think it was very likely.

Then Mama seemed to come to a decision.

"I'll tell you what we'll do," she said. "It's only two months till Christmas. Will you try just once more? Then if by Christmas you really feel you still can't manage, we'll do something about it. I don't quite know what, because we have no money for school fees, but I promise you I'll think of something. All right?"

"All right," said Anna.

The cake really was remarkably good, and by the time she had finished the last lick of chestnut purée she felt a lot less like Grete than before. They stayed sitting at the little table for a while longer because it was such a pleasant place to be.

"Nice to go out to tea with my daughter," said Mama at last and smiled.

Anna smiled back.

The bill came to more than they had expected and there was not enough money left for the cod after all, but Mama bought mussels instead and it did not matter. In the morning she gave Anna a note to Madame Socrate to explain about the home-work and she must have put something else in it as well, for Madame Socrate told Anna not to worry about school and also found time again to help her during the lunch break.

After this the work did not seem quite so bad. Whenever it threatened to overwhelm her, Anna remembered that if she really found it impossible she would not have to go on trying for ever, and then she usually discovered that she could manage after all.

And then, one day, her whole world changed.

It was a Monday morning and Colette met Anna at the school gates.

"What did you do on Sunday?" she called—and instead of mentally translating the question into German, deciding on an answer and then translating that back into French, Anna called back, "We went to see our friends."

The words just seemed to arrive from nowhere, in perfect French, without her having to think at all. She was so astonished that she stood quite still and did not even hear Colette's next question.

"I said," shouted Colette, "did you take the cat out?"

"No, it was too wet," said Anna—again in perfect French and without thinking.

It was like a miracle. She could not believe that it would last. It was as though she had suddenly found that she could fly, and she expected each moment to crash to the ground again. With her heart beating faster than usual she went into the classroom—but her new talent persisted.

In the first lesson she answered four questions correctly, so that Madame Socrate looked at her in surprise and said, "Well done!" She chattered and laughed with Colette in break and during lunch she explained to Clothilde how Mama cooked liver and onions. Once or twice she still hesitated, and of course she made mistakes. But most of the time she was able to speak French just as she spoke German—automatically and without thinking. By the end of the day she was almost light-headed with excitement but not at all tired, and when she woke up the next morning she had a moment of utter terror. Suppose her new gift had vanished as suddenly as it had come? But she need not have worried. When she got to school she found that she was even more fluent than before.

By the end of the week Mama looked at her in amazement.

"I've never seen such a change in anyone," she said. "A few days ago you looked green and miserable. Now it's as though you'd grown five centimetres and you look quite pink. What's happened to you?"

"I think I've learned to speak French," said Anna.

Chapter Twenty

There was even less money to spend at Christmas than the previous year, but it was more fun because of the Fernands. The main celebration in France is not at Christmas but on New Year's Eve when even the children are allowed to stay up till midnight, and they all had a special dinner and exchanged 'presents at the Fernands' flat. Anna had used some of her pocket money to buy some chocolate as a present for the white cat and after dinner, instead of playing with Max and Francine, she stayed behind in the living-room to feed it small crumbs of chocolate on the floor. Mama and Madame Fernand were washing up the dishes in the kitchen and Papa and Monsieur Fernand were drinking brandy and having one of their endless conversations, deep in two armchairs.

Papa seemed very interested in what they were talking about, and Anna was pleased because ever since that morning when a postcard had arrived from Onkel Julius, he had been silent and depressed. There had been postcards from Onkel Julius at irregular intervals throughout the year and though there was never any real news in them they were always full of affection. Sometimes there were little jokes and always there were messages for "Aunt Alice" to which Papa replied. This card had been addressed to Anna as usual but there was no mention of "Aunt Alice"—not even any good wishes for the New Year. Instead, on the back of a picture of some bears, Onkel Julius had simply written, "The more I see of men the more I love animals." He had not even initialled it as usual, but they knew it was from him because of his beautiful neat handwriting.

Papa had read it without a word and then had put it with the rest of Onkel Julius's cards and letters which he kept carefully in his table drawer. He had hardly spoken for the rest of the day, and now it was good to see him as animated as Monsieur Fernand.

"But you live in a free country," he was saying. "Nothing else matters!"

"Yes, but . . ." said Monsieur Fernand, and Anna realised that he must be worrying about the Depression again.

The Depression was the only thing that ever got Monsieur Fernand down, and though Anna had asked several times what it was no one had been able to explain it to her. It was something that had happened in France, and it meant that there was less money for everyone and fewer jobs, and it had caused some of Monsieur Fernand's colleagues to be sacked from his paper. Whenever Monsieur Fernand talked about the Depression Papa reminded him that he lived in a free country and this time, perhaps because of Onkel Julius, Papa was more eloquent than usual.

Monsieur Fernand argued with him for a while and then he suddenly laughed. The white cat opened its mouth in surprise at the noise and a crumb of chocolate fell out. When Anna looked up Monsieur Fernand was refilling Papa's glass and patting him on the shoulder.

"It's a funny thing," he said, "you trying to point out the more cheerful aspects of the situation, when you've got more to worry about than any of the rest of us!"

Then Mama and Madame Fernand came back into the room and soon it was midnight and everyone, even the children, drank a toast to the New Year.

"Happy 1935!" cried Monsieur Fernand, and "Happy 1935!" echoed everyone.

"To us and to all our friends," said Papa quietly, and Anna knew that he was thinking of Onkel Julius.

In February Mama caught 'flu and just as she was getting better the concierge developed a bad leg, which was very unfortunate. Since Grete's departure Mama had done most of the cleaning herself, but the concierge had come up for an hour each morning to help with the rough work. Now Mama was left with the lot. She did not like housework at the best of times and was feeling gloomy, as people tend to do after 'flu, and the burden of all the cleaning and cooking and washing and ironing and mending seemed to her simply too heavy to be borne. Anna and Max helped by doing odd jobs like shopping and emptying the dustbin, but of course most of the work fell back on Mama and she grumbled about it incessantly.

"I don't mind the cooking," she said, "but it's the endless washing and ironing and mending—it takes so long and it goes on for ever!"

Papa was no help at all. He had no idea what needed to be done in a household and when Mama complained how tired she got ironing the sheets he seemed genuinely astonished.

"But why do you bother?" he asked. "They get crumpled again anyway when people sleep in them."

"Oh, you don't understand anything!" cried Mama.

She felt extra bad about it because Omama was planning a visit to Great-Aunt Sarah and she wanted the flat to look nice when she came to see it. But while she cleaned the rooms—and Mama cleaned them with a kind of ferocity which they had never encountered from either Grete or the concierge—the washing accumulated, and while she cooked good and inexpensive meals the pile of mending grew and grew. Because Papa seemed quite unable to understand her difficulties she somehow felt that he was to blame and one evening they had a row.

Mama was trying to mend an old vest of Anna's and groaning a good deal because there was a pile of socks and pillow-cases waiting to be darned after she had finished, when Papa spoke.

"Surely this is quite unnecessary," he said. "There can be no real need to mend the children's underwear when no one ever sees it!"

He might have known, thought Anna, that this would cause an explosion.

"You have no idea—but no idea—" shouted Mama, "of the work I have to do. I get worn out washing and cooking and ironing and mending, and all you ever say is that it isn't necessary!"

"Only because you complain so much," said Papa. "After all other people seem to manage. Look at Madame Fernand."

This provoked another outburst.

"Madame Fernand loves housework!" shouted Mama. "Also she has a daily woman and a sewing machine. Look at this," she cried, waving a torn pillow-slip. "She'd be able to mend this in two minutes, whereas it'll take me at least half an hour. If you compare me with her it just shows you have no idea what you're talking about!"

Papa was taken aback by her vehemence. He loved Mama and hated to see her distressed.

"I only meant," he said, "that for an intelligent person like you there must be ways of simplifying . . ."

"Then you'd better ask Madame Fernand!" shouted Mama. "All I ever learned to do was how to play the piano!"—and she walked out of the room and slammed the door.

The following day when Anna came home from school she met Papa in the lift. He was carrying a large wooden box with a handle.

158

"What is it?" asked Anna and Papa said, "A present for Mama."

Anna was all agog to see what it was and could hardly wait for it to be opened, but Mama's face fell at the sight of it.

"Surely you haven't bought . . ." she began, as Papa lifted the lid, and Papa said proudly, "A sewing machine!"

It was not a bit like Madame Fernand's sewing machine, thought Anna. Madame Fernand's sewing machine was silver but this one was greyish black and a peculiar shape.

"Of course it's not new," said Papa, "and it may need to be cleaned. But you'll be able to mend the pillow-cases and socks with it, and make the children's clothes without asking Madame Fernand . . ."

"I don't know how to make clothes," said Mama, "and you can't mend socks with a sewing machine." She looked absolutely horrified.

"Well, whatever it is you do with a sewing machine," said Papa.

They all stared at the thing on the table. It did not look, thought Anna, as if it would do anything.

"How much did it cost?" asked Mama.

"Don't worry about that," said Papa. "They paid me for that extra article I wrote for the *Daily Parisian* today."

At this Mama became quite frantic.

"But we need that money!" she cried. "Don't you remember? I have to pay the rent and the butcher, and Anna needs new shoes. We said we'd use the money from the article to pay for them!"

Papa looked distressed. Clearly he had not remembered about these things, but before Mama could say any more the bell rang and Anna opened the door to Madame Fernand. In the excitement over the sewing machine everyone had forgotten that she was due to drop in for tea.

"Look!" cried Mama and Papa, but in very different tones of voice, as Anna led her into the dining-room.

Madame Fernand looked at the machine incredulously.

"Where on earth did you get it?" she said. "It must be out of the Ark!"

"Is it so old?" said Papa.

Madame Fernand inspected the machine more closely.

"Did you buy it?" she asked, still sounding astonished.

"Certainly!" said Papa.

"But the needle-plate—it's broken," said Madame Fernand. "And the whole shaft is bent sideways—someone must have dropped it—so that it couldn't possibly work."

She noticed some raised marks on the side of the machine and rubbed at them with her handkerchief. Gradually some figures appeared from beneath the grime. They formed a date—1896. Madame Fernand put her handkerchief back in her pocket.

"As an antique it may be interesting," she said firmly, "but as a sewing machine it's got to go back to the shop."

Papa still could not believe that his wonderful present was no use.

"Are you sure?" he asked.

"Quite sure," said Madame Fernand. "Take it quickly and tell them to give you your money back."

"And then will I be able to have new shoes?" asked Anna. She knew it wasn't really the moment to ask about them, but her old ones were quite worn out, apart from pinching her toes, and she had been looking forward to a new pair for a long time.

"Of course, of course," said Mama impatiently, but Papa still hesitated.

"I hope they'll agree," he said. "The man who sold it to me did not seem very helpful."

"I'll come with you," said Madame Fernand. "I want to see this place where they sell antique sewing machines," and Anna went along too.

The shop did not sell sewing machines only as Anna had expected but all sorts of different things like old chairs and little rickety tables and cracked pictures. Some of these had been put out on the pavement and a small ill-dressed man was busy draping a balding tiger skin over a chest of drawers in the middle. When he saw Papa his eyes, which were strangely pale, half closed.

"Good afternoon," said Papa politely as always. "I bought this sewing machine earlier today but I'm afraid it doesn't work."

"Doesn't it?" said the man, but he did not seem very surprised.

"No," said Papa. "So I've brought it back."

The man said nothing.

"And I'd be glad if you would be so kind as to refund the money."

"Ah, no!" said the man. "I can't do that. A bargain's a bargain."

"But the machine does not work," said Papa.

"Look, sir," said the man, momentarily abandoning the tiger skin. "You came in here and bought a sewing machine. Now you've changed your mind and you want your money back. Well, I don't do business that way. A bargain's a bargain, and that's all there is to it."

"I quite agree," said Papa, "that a bargain is a bargain. But the machine is broken."

"Where?" said the man.

Papa pointed vaguely.

The man dismissed it.

"Few little bits out of order," he said. "Cost you almost nothing to replace those. After all, you can't expect it to be perfect—not at the price you paid for it."

"No, I suppose not," said Papa, "but since it does not work at all, don't you think you should take it back?"

"No, I don't," said the man.

Papa seemed at a loss what to say next and Anna could see the money for her new shoes slipping away. She knew that Papa had been cheated but she also knew that he had meant it all for the best and that he was not the sort of person who could force the man to hand back the money. She sighed—but she had reckoned without Madame Fernand.

"Now you listen to me!" she shouted so loudly that several

passers-by turned round to look at her. "You've sold this man a wreck of a sewing machine while giving him to understand that it works. That's an offence against the law. I intend to inform the police immediately and I have no doubt they will also be most interested in all the other junk you sell here."

"Now, lady—please!" cried the man. His eyes were suddenly wide open.

"Don't tell me you came by this stuff honestly!" shouted Madame Fernand, giving the tiger skin a contemptuous tug. "There's nothing honest about your business! When the police have finished with you my husband, who is a journalist, will expose you in his paper . . ."

"Please, lady!" cried the man again, digging in his pocket. "Just a little misunderstanding!" And he hurriedly handed Papa some notes from a grubby wallet.

"Is that the right amount?" asked Madame Fernand sternly.

"It appears to be," said Papa.

"Then we'll go," she said.

They had only walked a few steps when the man came running after them.

What was it now? thought Anna nervously.

The man pointed apologetically.

"Excuse me, sir, but would you mind?" he said.

Papa looked down and discovered that he was still carrying the sewing machine in his hand. He put it down quickly. "I am terribly sorry," he said. "I am afraid I was a little confused."

"Of course, sir. Very natural, sir," said the man with no conviction whatever.

When Anna looked back a moment later he was gloomily arranging the sewing machine on top of the tiger skin.

They accompanied Madame Fernand to her Metro station.

"Now let's have no more nonsense about sewing machines," she said before she left them. "You know you can borrow mine any time you like. And tell your mother," she added to Anna, "that I'll drop in tomorrow and give her a hand with the mending."

She looked at Papa with a kind of admiration.

"You two," she said. "You must be the two most impractical people in the world!"

Anna and Papa walked home together. It was cold, but the sky was a bright, clear blue, and though there was no sign yet of spring there was a feeling that it was not too far away. At school that morning Anna had got seven out of ten for her dictation—only three mistakes. The money for her new shoes was safe in Papa's pocket. She was very happy.

Chapter Twenty-One

Omama arrived at Great-Aunt Sarah's just before Easter and came to see Mama and the children the following afternoon. With the help of the concierge (whose leg was now better) Mama had cleaned and tidied the flat so that it looked as nice as possible, but nothing could disguise the fact that it was very small and sparsely furnished.

"Can't you find anywhere bigger?" asked Omama while they were all having tea on the red oilcloth in the dining-room.

"A bigger flat would cost more," said Mama, helping Omama to some home-made apple flan. "We can barely afford this."

"But surely your husband . . .?" Omama seemed quite surprised.

"It's the Depression, Mother," said Mama. "Surely you've read about it! With so many French writers out of work no

French paper is going to engage a German to write for them, and the *Daily Parisian* can't afford to pay very much."

"Yes, but even so . . ." Omama looked round the little room, rather rudely, thought Anna, for after all it wasn't as bad as all that—and at that very moment Max, tilting his chair as usual, collapsed on the floor with a plateful of apple flan in his lap. ". . . This is no way for children to grow up," Omama finished her sentence, exactly as though Max had crystallised the thought for her.

Anna and Max burst into uncontrollable laughter, but Mama said, "Nonsense, Mother!" quite sharply and told Max to go and get himself cleaned up. "As a matter of fact the children are doing extremely well," she told Omama and added when Max was safely out of the room, "Max is working for the first time in his life."

"And I'm going to take the *certificat d'études!*" said Anna. This was her big news. Madame Socrate had decided, since her work had improved so much, that there was now no reason why she shouldn't take the examination in the summer with the rest of the class.

"The *certificat d'études?*" said Omama. "Isn't that some kind of elementary school examination?"

"It's for French twelve-year-old children," said Mama, "and Anna's teacher thinks it remarkable that she should have caught up so quickly."

But Omama shook her head.

"It all seems very strange to me," she said and looked sadly at Mama. "So very different from the way you were brought up."

She had bought presents for everyone and during the rest of her stay in Paris, as in Switzerland, she arranged several outings for Mama and the children which they enjoyed and would never normally have been able to afford. But she did not really understand their new life.

"This is no way for children to grow up" became a sort of catch-phrase in the family.

"This is no way for children to grow up!" Max would say

reproachfully to Mama when she had forgotten to make his sandwiches for school, and Anna would shake her head and say, "This is no way for children to grow up!" when the concierge caught Max sliding down the banisters.

After one of Omama's visits Papa, who usually managed to avoid meeting her, asked Mama, "How was your Mother?" and Anna heard Mama reply, "Kind and utterly unimaginative as usual."

When it was time for Omama to go back to the South of France she embraced Mama and the children fondly.

"Remember now," she told Mama, "if ever you're in difficulties you can send the children to me."

Anna caught Max's eye and mouthed, "This is no way for children to grow up!" and though it seemed mean in the face of all Omama's kindness they both had to make terrible grimaces to stop themselves from bursting into giggles.

After the Easter holidays Anna could hardly wait to go back to school. She loved it all since she had learned to speak French. Suddenly the work seemed quite easy and she was beginning to enjoy writing stories and compositions in French. It was not a bit like writing in German—you could make the words do quite different things—and she found it curiously exciting.

Even home-work was no longer such a burden. The large lumps of French, history and geography which had to be learned by heart were the hardest part, but Anna and Max had discovered a way of mastering even this. If they studied the relevant passage last thing before going to sleep they found they always knew it in the morning. By the afternoon it began to fade and by the following day it was completely forgotten— but it stuck in their memories just as long as they needed it.

One evening Papa came into their bedroom when they were hearing each others' lessons. Anna's was about Napoleon and Papa looked amazed as she reeled it off. It began "Napoleon was born in Corsica" and then followed a long list of dates and battles until the final "he died in 1821."

"What an extraordinary way to learn about Napoleon," said Papa. "Is that all you know about him?"

"But it's everything!" said Anna, rather hurt, especially as she had not made a single mistake.

Papa laughed. "No, it's not everything," he said, and settling down on her bed he began to talk about Napoleon. He told the children about Napoleon's childhood in Corsica with his many brothers and sisters, about his brilliance at school and how he became an officer at fifteen and commander of the entire French army at the age of twenty-six; how he made his brothers and sisters kings and queens of the countries he conquered but could never impress his mother, an Italian peasant woman.

"*C'est bien pourvu que ça dure,*" she would say disapprovingly at the news of every new triumph, which meant, "It's good as long as it lasts".

Then he told them how her forebodings came true, how half the French army was destroyed in the disastrous campaign against Russia, and finally of Napoleon's lonely death on the tiny island of St. Helena.

Anna and Max listened entranced.

"It's just like a film," said Max.

"Yes," said Papa thoughtfully. "Yes, it is."

It was nice, thought Anna, that Papa had more time to talk to them these days. This was because owing to the Depression the *Daily Parisian* had been reduced in size and could no longer print so many of his articles. But Mama and Papa did not think it was a good thing at all and Mama, in particular, was always worrying about money.

"We can't go on like this!" Anna once heard her say to Papa. "I always knew we should have gone to England in the first place."

But Papa only shrugged his shoulders and said, "It'll sort itself out."

Soon after this Papa became very busy again and Anna could hear him typing till late at night in his room, so she assumed that it had indeed "sorted itself out" and stopped thinking about it. She was, in any case, much too interested in school to pay much attention to what was happening at home. The *certificat d'études* loomed ever larger and closer and she was determined to pass it. After only a year and nine months in France she thought this would be a very splendid thing.

At last the day arrived and early one hot morning in July Madame Socrate led her class through the streets to a neighbouring school. They were to take the exam supervised by strange teachers so as to make it quite fair. It had all to be got through in one day, so there was not much time for each of the many subjects they were to be examined in. There was French, arithmetic, history, geography, singing, sewing, art and gym.

Arithmetic came first—an hour's paper in which Anna thought she acquitted herself quite well, then French dictation, then a ten-minute break.

"How did you get on?" Anna asked Colette.

"All right," said Colette.

So far it had not been too bad.

After break they were given two papers of questions on history and geography, each lasting half an hour, and then—disaster!

"As we are a little short of time," announced the teacher in charge, "it has been decided that this year, instead of examining candidates in both sewing and art, and adding the marks together as in previous years, you will be examined in sewing only and that this will count as a whole subject."

Sewing was what Anna was worst at. She could never remember the names of the different stitches and, perhaps because Mama was so bad at it, she thought the whole business was an awful waste of time. Even Madame Socrate had never been able to persuade her to become interested in it. She had cut out an apron for her to hem, but Anna had been so slow at getting on with it that by the time it was finished she had grown too tall to wear it.

The teacher's pronouncement therefore plunged her into

168

deep gloom which was confirmed when she was given a square of material, a needle and thread and some incomprehensible instructions. For half an hour she guessed wildly, tore her thread and picked frantically at knots which seemed to appear from nowhere, and finally handed in a piece of sewing so ragged and crumpled that even the teacher collecting it looked startled at the sight of it.

Lunch in the school playground with Colette was a glum affair.

"If you fail one subject, do you automatically fail the whole exam?" Anna asked as they sat eating their sandwiches on a bench in the shade.

"I'm afraid so," said Colette, "unless you get distinctions in another subject—then that makes up for it."

Anna ran through the exams she had already taken in her mind. Except for sewing she had done well in them all—but not well enough to have got distinctions. Her chances of passing seemed very slender.

However, she cheered up a little when she saw the subjects set for French composition in the afternoon. There were three to chose from and one of them was "A journey". Anna decided to describe what she imagined Papa's journey must have been like when he had travelled from Berlin to Prague with a high temperature, not knowing whether or not he would be stopped at the frontier. There was a whole hour allowed for it and as she wrote Papa's journey became more and more vivid to her. She felt she knew exactly what it must have been like, what Papa's thoughts must have been and how, owing to the temperature, he would keep getting confused between what he was thinking and what was actually happening. By the time Papa had arrived in Prague she had written nearly five pages, and she just had time to check them through for punctuation and spelling before they were collected. She thought it was one of the best compositions she had ever written, and if only it had not been for the beastly sewing she would be sure now of having passed.

The only exams still to come were singing and gym. The

singing tests were held separately for each child but as time was getting short they were very brief.

"Sing the *Marseillaise*," commanded the teacher but stopped Anna after the first few bars. "Good—that will do," she said and then cried, "Next!"

There were only ten minutes left for gym.

"Quickly! Quickly!" cried the teacher as she herded the children into the playground and told them to spread out. There was another teacher to help her, and together they arranged the children in four long lines a metre or two apart.

"Attention!" cried one of the teachers. "Everyone stand on your right leg with your left leg raised off the ground in front of you!"

Everyone did, except Colette who stood on her left leg by mistake and had surreptitiously to change over. Anna stood dead straight, her arms held out to balance herself and her left leg raised as high as she could. Out of the corner of her eye she could see some of the others, and nobody's leg was as high off the ground as her own. The two teachers walked between the lines of children, some of whom were now beginning to wobble and collapse, and made notes on a piece of paper. When they came to Anna they stopped.

"Very good!" said one of them.

"Really excellent," said the other. "Don't you think . . .?"

"Oh, definitely!" said the first teacher, and made a mark on the piece of paper.

"That's it! You can go home now!" they called when they got to the end of the line, and Colette rushed up to Anna and embraced her.

"You've done it! You've done it!" she cried. "You've got distinctions in gym, so now it won't matter if you've failed in sewing!"

"Do you really think so?" said Anna, but she felt pretty sure of it herself.

She walked home through the hot streets glowing with happiness and could hardly wait to tell Mama all about it.

"You mean to say that because you were so good at standing

on one leg it won't matter that you can't sew?" said Mama. "What an extraordinary exam!"

"I know," said Anna, "but I suppose it's things like French and arithmetic that are really important and I think I did quite well in those."

Mama had made some cold lemon squash and they sat drinking it together in the dining-room while Anna rattled on. "We should have the results in a few days' time—it can't be much more because it's nearly the end of term. Wouldn't it be grand if I'd really passed—after less than two years in France!"

Mama agreed that it would indeed be grand, when the door bell rang and Max appeared looking pale and excited.

"Mama," he said almost before he had got through the door. "You've got to come to the prize-giving on Saturday. If you've got anything else on you've got to cancel it. It's very important!"

Mama looked very pleased.

"Have you won the Latin prize then?" she asked.

But Max shook his head.

"No," he said, and the rest of the sentence seemed somehow to stick in his throat. "I've won . . ." he said, and finally brought out, "I've won the *prix d'excellence!* That means they think I'm the best student in the class."

Of course there was delight and praise from everyone. Even Papa was interrupted in his typing to hear the great news, and Anna thought it was just as wonderful as everyone else. But she could not help wishing that it had not come just at this very moment. She had worked so hard and thought so long about passing the *certificat d'études*. After this, even if she did pass, how could anyone possibly be impressed? Especially since her success would be partly due to her talent for standing on one leg?

When the results were announced it was not nearly as exciting as she had expected. She had passed, so had Colette and so had most of the class. Madame Socrate handed each successful candidate an envelope containing a certificate with her name on it. But when Anna opened hers she found something more. Attached to the certificate were two ten franc notes and a letter from the Mayor of Paris.

"What does it mean?" she asked Madame Socrate.

Madame Socrate's wrinkled face broke into a delighted smile.

"The Mayor of Paris has decided to award prizes for the twenty best French compositions written by children taking the *certificat d'études*," she explained. "It seems that you have been awarded one of them."

When Anna told Papa he was just as pleased as he had been about Max's *prix d'excellence*.

"It's your first professional fee as a writer," he said. "It's really remarkable to have earned it in a language not your own."

Chapter Twenty-Two

The summer holidays arrived and Anna suddenly realised that no one had said anything about going away. It was very hot. You could feel the heat of the pavement through the soles of your shoes and the sun seemed to soak deep into the streets and the houses, so that they did not cool even at night. The Fernands had left for the seaside right after the end of term, and as July turned into August Paris gradually emptied. The paper shop at the corner was the first to put up a sign saying "Closed until September" but several others soon followed. Even the owner of the shop where Papa had bought the sewing machine had put up his shutters and gone away.

It was difficult to know what to do during the long hot days. The flat was stifling, and even in the shady square where Anna and Max usually played the heat was too great for them to do anything very interesting. They would throw a ball about or play with their spinning tops for a while, but they soon became tired and sank on to a seat to dream of swimming and cold drinks.

"Wouldn't it be lovely," said Anna, "if we were sitting by the edge of Lake Zurich and could just jump in!"

Max pulled at his shirt where it had stuck to his skin.

"It's not likely to happen," he said. "We've hardly enough money to pay the rent, let alone go away."

"I know," said Anna. But it sounded so gloomy that she added, "Unless someone buys Papa's film script."

Papa's film script had been inspired by his conversation with the children about Napoleon. It was not about Napoleon himself but about his mother—how she had brought up her children without any money, how all their lives were changed by Napoleon's success and how at last she outlived him, an old blind lady, long after his final defeat. It was the first film script Papa had ever written and he had been working on it when Anna imagined that things had "sorted themselves out" with the *Daily Parisian*. Since the paper was now in greater difficulties than ever she hoped that the film would make Papa's fortune instead—but up to now there had been little sign of it.

Two French film companies to whom Papa had shown it had returned it with depressing speed. Finally Papa had sent it to a Hungarian film director in England, and this seemed an even less likely bet since it was not known for certain whether the Hungarian could read German. Also, thought Anna, why should the English, who had been Napoleon's greatest enemies, be more eager to make a film about him than the French? But at least the script had not yet come back, so there was still hope.

"I don't really think anyone's going to buy that film, do you?" said Max. "And I don't know what Papa and Mama are going to do for money."

"Oh, something will turn up," said Anna, but secretly she was a little frightened. Suppose nothing turned up. What then?

Mama was more irritable than they had ever known her.

Quite small things seemed to upset her, like the time when Anna had broken her hairslide.

"Why couldn't you have been more careful?" Mama had stormed, and when Anna pointed out that the hairslide only cost thirty centimes, Mama had shouted, "Thirty centimes is thirty centimes!" and had insisted on trying to glue the hairslide together again before buying a new one. Once she had said, out of the blue, "How would you children like to stay with Omama for a while?"

Max had answered, "Not at all!" and they had all laughed, but afterwards it did not seem so funny.

At night in the dark, hot bedroom Anna worried what would happen if Papa's financial situation did not improve. Would she and Max really be sent away?

Halfway through August a letter arrived from England. It was signed by the Hungarian film director's secretary. She said that the Hungarian film director thanked Papa for the script and that he looked forward to reading anything written by so distinguished an author, but that he felt he must warn Papa of the general lack of interest in films about Napoleon at present.

Mama, who had got quite excited at the sight of the English stamp, was deeply disappointed.

"He's had it nearly a month and he hasn't even read it yet!" she cried. "If only we were in England! Then we could do something about it!"

"I can't think what," said Papa—but lately "if only we were in England" had become Mama's constant cry. It was not only because of the nice English governess she had had as a child, but she kept hearing of other refugees who had settled in England and found interesting work. She hated the French papers for not asking Papa to write for them and she hated the French film companies for rejecting his film, and most of all she hated being always so short of money that even the purchase of small necessities like a new tube of toothpaste became a major worry.

About two weeks after the letter from England, things came

to a head. It began when something went wrong with Mama's bed. She was trying to make it after breakfast, and when she had packed the sheets and pillows away and was about to turn it back into a sofa, it suddenly stuck. The padded seat-cum-mattress which was supposed to slide over the bedding refused to move. She called Max to help her and they both pushed, but it was no use. The seat stuck obstinately out into the room while Mama and Max mopped their faces, for it was already very hot. "Oh, why does something always have to go wrong!" cried Mama and then added, "The concierge will have to fix it. Anna, run and ask her to come up."

This was not a very attractive task. Recently, in order to save money, Mama had terminated the arrangement by which the concierge came up each day to help with the cleaning, and now the concierge was always very bad-tempered. But fortunately Anna met her just outside the door.

"I've brought up the mail," said the concierge—it was only a circular—"and I've come for the rent."

"Good morning, Madame," said Papa politely as always, meeting the concierge in the hall, and, "Could you have a look at this bed?" asked Mama as the concierge followed Anna into her room.

The concierge gave the bed a perfunctory push.

"I expect the children have been messing about with it," she said and then repeated, "I've come for the rent."

"The children haven't been near it," said Mama crossly, "and what's all this about the rent? It's not due till tomorrow."

"Today," said the concierge.

"But it's not the first of September."

In reply the concierge pointed silently to the date on a newspaper she was carrying in her hand.

"Oh, very well," said Mama and called to Papa, "It's the rent."

"I didn't realise it was due today," said Papa. "I'm afraid I shall have to give it to you tomorrow," whereupon a peculiarly unpleasant expression came over the concierge's face.

Mama looked worriedly at Papa.

"But I don't understand," she said quickly in German. "Didn't you go to the *Daily Parisian* yesterday?"

"Of course," said Papa, "but they asked me to wait until this morning."

Recently the *Daily Parisian* had been in such difficulties that the editor sometimes found it hard to pay Papa even for the few articles that he was able to publish, and just now he owed him for three of them.

"I don't know what you're talking about to each other," the concierge interrupted rudely, "but the rent is due today. Not tomorrow but today."

Both Mama and Papa were surprised by her tone.

"You'll get your rent," said Mama, the colour rising in her face. "Now will you please fix this ramshackle contraption so that I shall have somewhere to sleep tonight!"

"Hardly worth my while, is it?" said the concierge, making no move to do so. "I mean—people who can't even pay the rent on time . . .!"

Papa looked very angry.

"I will not have you talk to my wife in that tone!" he said, but the concierge was unimpressed.

"Giving yourself airs," she said, "with nothing to show for it!"

At this Mama lost her temper.

"Will you please fix this bed!" she shouted. "And if you can't fix it, get out!"

"Ha!" said the concierge. "Hitler knew what he was doing when he got rid of people like you!"

"Get out!" shouted Papa and pushed the concierge towards the front door.

As she went through Anna heard her say, "The government should have had more sense than to let you into our country!"

When they went back to Mama she was standing motionless, staring at the bed. There was an expression on her face which Anna had never seen, and as Papa came in she shouted, "We can't go on like this!" and gave the bed a tremendous kick.

It must have dislodged something, for all at once the padded seat shot forward across the frame and closed with a bang. At this everyone laughed except Mama, who suddenly became very calm.

"It's Thursday," she said in an abnormally quiet voice, "so there'll be a children's matinee at the cinema." She searched in her purse and handed Max some money. "You two go."

"Are you sure?" said Max. The children's matinees were a franc each and for some time now Mama had said they were much too expensive.

"Yes, yes," said Mama. "Go quickly or you'll be late for the beginning."

There was something that did not feel right about it, but it was too big a treat to miss. So Anna and Max went to the cinema and watched three cartoons, a newsreel and a film about deep-sea fishing. When they returned they found everything normal. Lunch was on the table and Mama and Papa were standing very close together by the window, talking.

"You'll be glad to hear," said Papa when the children came in, "that the monstrous concierge has been paid her rent. I extracted my dues from the *Daily Parisian*."

"But we must have a talk," said Mama.

They waited while she dished out the food.

"We can't go on like this," said Mama. "You can see that for yourselves. It's impossible for Papa to earn a decent living in this country. So Papa and I think the only thing is to go to England, to see if we can start a new life there."

"When would we go?" asked Anna.

"Only Papa and I would go to start with," said Mama. "You and Max would go to stay with Omama and Opapa until we get things sorted out."

Max looked depressed but nodded. Clearly he had been expecting this.

"But supposing it took you quite a long time to get things sorted out," said Anna. "We wouldn't see you."

"It just wouldn't have to take us too long," said Mama.

"But Omama . . ." said Anna. "I know she's very kind,

178

but . . ." She couldn't very well say that Omama did not like Papa, so she asked Papa instead, "What do you think?"

Papa's face had the tired look that Anna hated, but he said quite firmly, "You'll be properly looked after there. And you'll go to school—your education won't be interrupted." He smiled. "You're both doing so well."

"It's the only thing to do," said Mama.

Something hard and unhappy rose inside Anna.

"Is it all settled, then?" she asked. "Don't you even want to know what we think?"

"Of course we do," said Mama, "but the way things are, we haven't much choice."

"Tell us what you think," said Papa.

Anna stared at the red oilcloth in front of her.

"It's just that I think we should stay together," she said. "I don't really mind where or how. I don't mind things being difficult, like not having any money, and I didn't mind about that silly concierge this morning—just as long as we're all four together."

"But Anna," said Mama, "lots of children leave their parents for a while. Lots of English children go to boarding schools."

"I know," said Anna, "but it's different if you haven't got a home. If you haven't got a home you've got to be with your people." She looked at her parents' stricken faces and burst out, "I know! I know we have no choice and I'm only making it more difficult. But I've never minded being a refugee before. In fact I've loved it. I think the last two years, when we've been refugees, have been much better than if we'd stayed in Germany. But if you send us away now I'm so terribly frightened . . . I'm so terribly frightened . . ."

"Of what?" asked Papa.

"That I might really feel like one!" said Anna and burst into tears.

Chapter Twenty-Three

Afterwards Anna was very ashamed of her outburst. After all she had really known all the time that Mama and Papa had no choice but to send her and Max away. All she had done was to make everyone feel worse about something that had to happen anyway. Why couldn't she have kept quiet? She worried about it in bed and when she woke up early the next morning she felt she must do something. She still had some of her prize money left—she would go out and buy croissants for everybody's breakfast.

There was a little breeze blowing for the first time in weeks and when she came back from the baker's with the hot croissants in a bag she suddenly felt much happier. It would all work out somehow—everything would be all right.

A man was talking to the concierge in a strong German accent and as she passed Anna heard him asking for Papa.

"I'll take you up," she said, disregarding the concierge, and the concierge, in offended silence, handed her a letter. Anna looked down at it and saw with a sudden quickening of the pulse that it had an English stamp. All the way up in the lift she could think of nothing but what might be inside the letter, and she only remembered Papa's visitor when he spoke to her.

"You must be Anna," he said and she nodded.

He was a shabby-looking man with a sad voice.

"Papa!" cried Anna as they entered the flat. "I've bought some croissants for breakfast and there's a letter and someone to see you!"

"Someone here? Now?" said Papa as he emerged from his room, tying his tie.

He drew the visitor into the dining-room and Anna followed with the letter in her hand.

"How do you do, Herr . . .?"

"Rosenfeld," said the man with a little bow. "I used to be an actor in Berlin but you don't know me. Only small parts, you understand." He smiled, showing irregular yellow teeth and added with apparent irrelevance, "I have a nephew in the confectionery business."

"Papa . . ." said Anna, holding out the letter, but Papa said, "Later!"

Herr Rosenfeld seemed to find it difficult to say what he had come for. His sad eyes kept roaming round the dining-room while he considered one opening after another and dismissed each one. At last he put his hand in his pocket and pulled out a small parcel wrapped in brown paper.

"I have brought you this," he said and handed it to Papa. Papa unwrapped it. It was a watch—an old silver watch—and there was something familiar about it.

"Julius!" cried Papa.

Herr Rosenfeld nodded sadly. "I am the bearer of bad news."

Onkel Julius was dead.

While Mama gave Herr Rosenfeld some coffee and he absent-mindedly nibbled one of Anna's croissants he told them how Onkel Julius had died. He had been dismissed from his post as curator of the Berlin Natural History Museum nearly a year ago.

"But why?" asked Mama.

"Surely you knew," said Herr Rosenfeld. "He had a Jewish grandmother."

Onkel Julius had not been able to work as a naturalist after this but had found a job sweeping up in a factory. He had moved from his flat into a cheap room, and this was where he had made friends with Herr Rosenfeld who had the room next-door. In spite of his difficulties Onkel Julius had been quite cheerful at this stage.

"He just . . . accepted things, didn't he?" said Herr Rosenfeld. "I was planning even then to come to Paris and join my nephew, and I said to him, 'You come too—there's room for us both in the confectionery trade!' But he wouldn't. He seemed to think that the situation in Germany was bound to change."

Papa nodded, remembering Onkel Julius in Switzerland.

Herr Rosenfeld and Onkel Julius had had many conversations together and Onkel Julius had talked a great deal about Papa and his family. Once or twice Herr Rosenfeld had accompanied him to the Zoo where he now spent all his Sundays. Though Onkel Julius had so little money he always managed to bring some peanuts for the monkeys and scraps for the other animals, and Herr Rosenfeld had been amazed to see how they rushed to the bars of their cages as soon as he appeared.

"It wasn't just the food," he said. "It was more like a sort of gentleness in him that they recognised."

Again Papa nodded . . .

During the autumn Onkel Julius had even dropped into the Zoo after work in the evenings. His whole life now centred round the animals. There was a monkey that let him stroke it through the bars of its cage . . .

And then, just before Christmas, the blow had fallen. Onkel Julius had received an official letter revoking his pass to the Zoo. No reason was given. The fact that he had a Jewish grandmother was enough.

After this Onkel Julius had changed. He could not sleep and did not eat properly. He no longer talked to Herr Rosenfeld but spent the Sundays in his room, staring at the sparrows on the roof-top opposite. At last, late one night in spring, he had knocked on Herr Rosenfeld's door and begged him, when he went to Paris, to take something to Papa. Herr Rosenfeld had explained that he would not be going for some time yet, but Onkel Julius had said, "Never mind, I'll give it to you now," and Herr Rosenfeld had accepted a small parcel to calm him. Next morning Onkel Julius had been found dead, an empty bottle of sleeping tablets beside him.

Herr Rosenfeld had not been able to leave Germany till several months later, but had at once come to see Papa and to deliver the parcel.

"There's a note as well," he said.

The handwriting was as meticulous as ever.

It said simply, "Good-bye. I wish you well," and was signed "Julius".

For quite a long time after Herr Rosenfeld had left Anna forgot about the other letter from England which she was still holding in her hand, but at last she remembered and gave it to Papa. He opened it, read it silently and passed it to Mama.

"They want to buy your film script!" cried Mama and then, as though she could hardly believe it, "A thousand pounds . . .!"

"Does that mean we don't have to go and stay with Omama?" Max asked quickly.

"Of course!" said Mama. "There's no need now for you to go away. We can all go to England together!"

"Oh Papa!" cried Anna. "Papa, isn't it wonderful!"

"Yes," said Papa. "I'm glad we shall all be together."

"To think that they're going to film your script!" Mama's hand was on his shoulder. Then she noticed the frayed collar under her fingers. "You'll need a new jacket," she said.

"Let's tell the concierge and give her notice!" said Max.

"No—wait!" cried Mama. "But if we're going to London, we ought to let your schools know. And we must find out about hotels. And it'll be colder there—you'll need some woollies . . ."

Suddenly there seemed to be a thousand things to talk about.

But Papa, who had made it all happen, did not want to talk about any of them. While Mama and the children chattered and made plans he sat quite still and let the words flow round him. Onkel Julius's watch was in his hand and he was stroking it, very gently, with one finger.

Chapter Twenty-Four

It seemed strange to be leaving again for yet another country.

"Just when we'd learned to speak French properly," said Max.

There was not time to say good-bye to Madame Socrate because she was still on holiday. Anna had to leave a note for her at the school. But she went with Mama to pay a farewell visit to Great-Aunt Sarah who wished them luck in their new life in England and was delighted to hear about Papa's film.

"At last someone is paying that good man some money," she said. "They should have done it long ago already."

The Fernands returned from the seaside just in time for the two families to spend a final evening together. Papa took everyone out to dinner to celebrate and they promised each other to meet again soon.

"We'll come back to France often," said Papa. He had a new jacket and the tired look had quite disappeared from his face.

"And you must visit us in London," said Mama.

"We'll come to see the film," said Madame Fernand.

The packing did not take long. There seemed to be less to pack each time they moved—so many things had been used up and thrown away—and one grey morning less than two weeks after the letter had come from England, they were ready to leave.

Mama and Anna stood in the little dining-room for the last time, waiting for the taxi to take them to the station. Cleared of the litter of small objects in everyday use which had made it familiar, the room looked bare and cheap.

"I don't know how we lived here for two years," said Mama.

Anna rubbed her hand over the red oil-cloth on the table.

"I liked it," she said.

Then the taxi came. Papa and Max piled the luggage into the lift and then Papa shut the door of the flat behind them.

When the train drew out of the station Anna leaned out of the window with Papa and watched Paris slowly slip away.

"We'll come back," said Papa.

"I know," said Anna. She remembered how she had felt when they had gone back to the Gasthof Zwirn for the holidays and added, "But it won't be the same—we won't belong. Do you think we'll ever really belong anywhere?"

"I suppose not," said Papa. "Not the way people belong who have lived in one place all their lives. But we'll belong a little in lots of places, and I think that may be just as good."

The equinoctial gales were early that year and when the train reached Dieppe about lunch-time the sea looked wild and dark under the grey sky. They had chosen the slow crossing from Dieppe to Newhaven because it was cheaper, in spite of Papa's new-found wealth.

"We don't know how long the money will have to last us," said Mama.

As soon as the boat emerged from Dieppe harbour it began

to pitch and roll and Anna's excitement at her first sea voyage quickly evaporated. She, Max and Mama watched each others' faces turn paler and greener until they had to go below and lie down. Only Papa was unaffected. It took six hours to cross the Channel instead of the customary four because of the bad weather, and long before they landed Anna felt that she did not care what England was like, just as long as they got there. When they finally arrived it was too dark to see anything. The boat train had left long ago and a kind but incomprehensible porter put them on a slow train to London instead.

As it started hesitantly on its way a spatter of raindrops appeared on the window.

"English weather," said Papa who was very cheerful because he had not been sea-sick.

Anna sat huddled in her corner of the compartment, watching the anonymous dark landscape rush past. You could not really see what any of it was like. After a while she got tired of looking at it and stole a glance, instead, at two men opposite her. They were English. In the rack above their heads were two black melon-shaped hats such as she had rarely seen before and they were sitting up very straight, reading newspapers. Although they had got on to the train together they did not speak to each other. The English seemed to be very quiet people.

The train slowed down and stopped, for the umpteenth time, at a small ill-lit station.

"Where are we?" asked Mama.

Anna spelled out the name on an illuminated sign.

"Bovril," she said.

"It can't be," said Max. "The last place we stopped at was called Bovril."

Mama, still pale from the crossing, looked for herself.

"It's an advertisement," she said. "Bovril is some kind of English food. I think they eat it with stewed fruit."

The train continued to crawl through the darkness and Anna became drowsy. There was something familiar about the situation—her tiredness, the sound of the train wheels, and the rain spattering on the windows. It had all happened before, some time long ago. Before she could remember when, she fell asleep.

When she awoke the train was going faster and there were lights flashing past the windows. She looked out and saw wet roads and street lamps and little houses which all looked alike.

"We're coming into London," said Mama.

The roads grew wider and the buildings bigger and more varied, and suddenly the sound of the wheels changed and they were on a bridge over a wide river.

"The Thames!" cried Papa.

It was lined with lights on both sides and Anna could see some cars and a red bus crawling along beneath them. Then they were across, the river was left behind, and as though a box had been clapped over the train, the brightness of a station with platforms and porters and crowds of people suddenly appeared all round them. They had arrived.

Anna climbed off the train and stood on the chilly platform while they waited for Mama's cousin Otto who was to meet them. All round them the English were greeting each other, smiling and talking.

"Can you understand what they're saying?" asked Anna.

"Not a word," said Max.

"A few months and we'll be able to," said Anna.

Papa had got hold of a porter, but Cousin Otto was nowhere to be seen, so Mama and Papa went to look for him while the children stayed with the luggage. It was cold. Anna sat down on a suitcase and the porter smiled at her.

"*Français?*" he asked.

Anna shook her head.

"*Deutsch?*"

She nodded.

"Ah, *Deutsch*," said the porter. He was a tubby little man with a red face. "Ittla?" he added.

Anna and Max looked at each other. They did not know what he meant.

"Ittla! Ittla!" said the porter. He placed one finger under his nose like a moustache and raised the other hand in the Nazi salute. "Ittla?" he said.

"Oh, Hitler!" cried Max.

Anna said, "Do they have Nazis here?"

"I hope not," said Max.

They both shook their heads vehemently and made disapproving faces.

"No!" they said. "No Hitler!"

The porter seemed pleased.

"Ittla . . ." he began. He looked round to see if anyone was watching him and then spat forcefully on the platform. "Ittla," he said. That was what he thought of him.

They all smiled and the porter was just about to do another imitation of Hitler with his hair pulled down over his forehead, when Mama appeared from one side and Papa and Cousin Otto from the other.

"Welcome to England!" cried Cousin Otto, embracing Mama. Then, as Mama gave a little shiver, he added reprovingly, "In this country you should always wear woollen underclothes."

Anna remembered him from Berlin as a rather dapper man, but now he looked shabby in a crumpled coat. They followed him to the exit in a slow procession. There were people all round them. It was so damp that steam seemed to be rising from the ground and Anna's nostrils were filled with the smell of rubber from the mackintoshes which nearly all the English were wearing. At the end of the platform there was a slight hold-up, but nobody pushed or jostled as was usual in France and Germany—everyone just waited their turn. Through the misty air a fruit stall shone bright with oranges, apples and yellow bananas and there was a shop window entirely filled with sweets and chocolates. The English must be very rich to be able to buy such things. They passed an English policeman with a tall helmet and another one in a wet cape.

Outside the station the rain was coming down like a shining curtain and beyond it Anna could dimly see some kind of

189

open square. Again the feeling came over her that this had all happened before. She had stood in the rain outside a station and it had been cold . . .

"Wait here and I'll get a taxi," said Cousin Otto, and this, too, was familiar.

Suddenly her tiredness and the bad crossing and the cold all combined. There was a great emptiness in her head and the rain seemed to be all about her and the past and the present became confused, so that for a moment she could not think where she was.

"All right?" said Papa, grasping her arm as she swayed a little, and Cousin Otto said in a concerned voice, "It must be quite difficult to spend one's childhood moving from country to country."

At the words something cleared in Anna's mind.

"Difficult childhood . . ." she thought. The past and the present slid apart. She remembered the long, weary journey from Berlin with Mama, how it had rained, and how she had read Gunther's book and wished for a difficult childhood so that she might one day become famous. Had her wish then come true? Could her life since she had left Germany really be described as a difficult childhood?

She thought of the flat in Paris and the Gasthof Zwirn. No, it was absurd. Some things had been difficult, but it had always been interesting and often funny—and she and Max and Mama and Papa had nearly always been together. As long as they were together she could never have a difficult childhood. She sighed a little as she abandoned her hopes.

"What a pity," she thought. "I'll never be famous at this rate!"

She moved closer to Papa and put her hand in his pocket for warmth.

Then Cousin Otto came back with the taxi.

"Quickly!" he cried. "He won't wait!"

They all ran. Papa and Cousin Otto shifted the luggage. The taxi driver threw it into the taxi. Mama slipped in the wet and almost fell, but Cousin Otto saved her.

"The English all wear rubber soles," he cried, pushing in the last suitcase.

Then they all piled into the taxi. Cousin Otto gave the address of the hotel. Anna pressed her face against the window, and the taxi started.